IRELAND
IN COLOUR

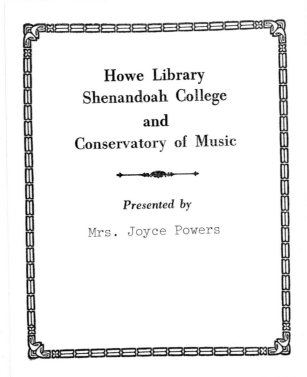

IRELAND
IN COLOUR

*A Collection
of Forty Colour Photographs*

*With an Introductory Text
and Notes on the Illustrations by*

W. R. RODGERS

HASTINGS HOUSE
Publishers
New York, 22

First published 1957
Reprinted 1963

PRINTED AND BOUND IN GREAT BRITAIN
BY JARROLD AND SONS LTD, LONDON AND NORWICH

CONTENTS

LIST OF ILLUSTRATIONS

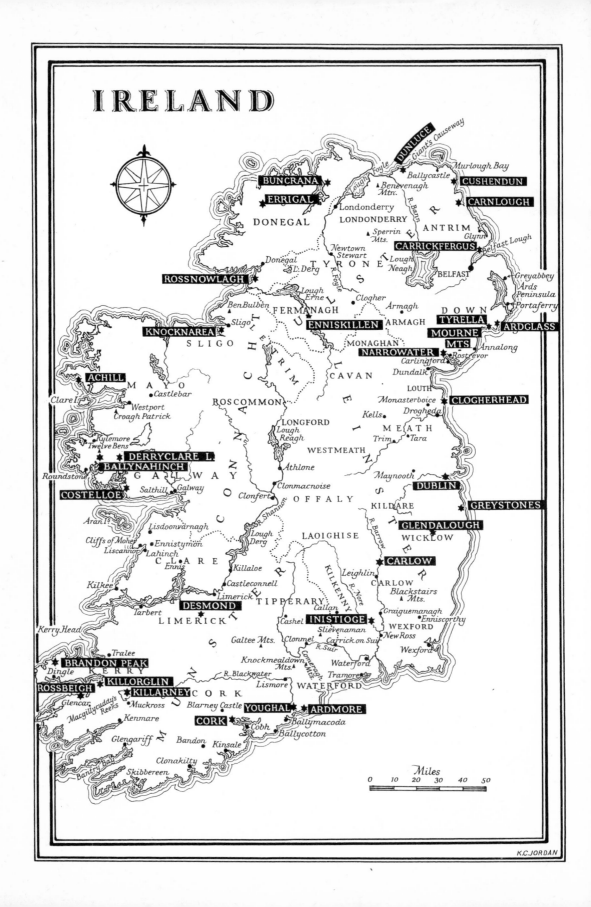

IRELAND

DUNLUCE
Giant's Causeway
Lough Foyle
Benevenagh Mtn.
Ballycastle
Murlough Bay
CUSHENDUN
BUNCRANA
ERRIGAL
CARNLOUGH
Londonderry
LONDONDERRY
ANTRIM
Glynn
DONEGAL
Sperrin Mts.
R. Bann
R. Foyle
CARRICKFERGUS
Belfast Lough
Donegal
L: Derg
T Y R O N E
Lough Neagh
Belfast
ROSSNOWLAGH
Lough Erne
Greyabbey
Ards Peninsula
Portaferry
Ben Bulben
FERMANAGH
Clogher
Armagh
D O W N
Sligo
ENNISKILLEN
ARMAGH
TYRELLA
MOURNE
Annalong
KNOCKNAREA
Monaghan
MONAGHAN
NARROWATER
MTS
Rostrevor
S L I G O
Carlingford
ACHILL
L E I T R I M
CAVAN
Dundalk
Clare I.
M A Y O
Castlebar
R O S C O M M O N
LOUTH
Monasterboice
Drogheda
CLOGHERHEAD
Westport
Croagh Patrick
Kells
M E A T H
Kylemore
Twelve Bens
Longford
LONGFORD
Lough Reagh
Trim
Tara
DERRYCLARE L.
WESTMEATH
BALLYNAHINCH
Roundstone
G A L W A Y
Athlone
Maynooth
Salthill
Galway
Clonmacnoise
DUBLIN
COSTELLOE
Clonfert
O F F A L Y
GREYSTONES
Aran Is.
Lisdoonvarnagh
Lough Derg
KILDARE
GLENDALOUGH
Cliffs of Moher
Ennistymon
LAOIGHISE
WICKLOW
Liscannor
Lahinch
C L A R E
R. Barrow
Ennis
CARLOW
Kilkee
Killaloe
Leighlin
Castleconnell
CARLOW
Limerick
T I P P E R A R Y
Blackstairs Mts.
DESMOND
KILKENNY
Graiguemanagh
Tarbert
Callan
Enniscorthy
LIMERICK
Cashel
INISTIOGE
WEXFORD
Kerry Head
Galtee Mts.
Clonmel
Slievenaman
New Ross
BRANDON PEAK
Knockmealdown Mts.
Carrick on Suir
Wexford
Tralee
R. Suir
KILLORGLIN
Dingle
K E R R Y
R. Blackwater
Waterford
Tramore
ROSSBEIGH
Lismore
WATERFORD
KILLARNEY
Glencar
C O R K
Muckross
Blarney Castle
YOUGHAL
ARDMORE
Macgillicuddy's Reeks
CORK
Ballymacoda
Kenmare
Cobh
Ballycotton
Glengariff
Bandon
Kinsale
Clonakilty
Bantry Bay
Skibbereen

Miles
0 10 20 30 40 50

K.C.JORDAN

I Emerald Isle

It's down by hazy pale slabs of water,
Through bushy towns we'll quietly go—
Just telling each hour by the change of colour
*On the mountains of Mayo.**

AN Englishman who breakfasted at a farmhouse in County Cork wondered to see the farmer's wife put all the eggs into the teapot to boil. He asked her about it. "Ah," said she, "sure don't they all come out the same colour, and then there's no fighting among the children for who'll get the brown one."

Ireland knows very well how to please her colourful children in matters of provender or politics. By nature hers are a dramatic people, loving clash and contrast, and their crying-out colour is not green but red. Over and over again, in the green glens and hills of Ireland, in the brown bog of her central plain, or in the vast stony silences of the western seaboard one is suddenly aware of a loud dot of red in the lonely landscape, the red of a petticoat or a shawl, that heightens and offsets every other tone. One sees it too in her cities. From the deck of the mail-boat docked in Dunlaoghaire, I look across the harbour on a fine sunny evening at the coloured yachts abounding like toys, dipping and bobbing in front of the grey Georgian houses. Over and beyond them a brown thunder-cloud fumes and cauliflowers up above the purple gloom of the Wicklow hills. But it is the mile-long pier in the foreground, strung with promenading sight-seers, and clustered with people listening to a brass band, that fascinates me. What is it, in this rainbow-tinted crowd that reminds me emphatically of the coloured postcards of my boyhood, when colours seemed more vivid than ever I have known them since? Partly, I think, it is the prevalent splashes of red in the scene. For where else in these islands would one see so many women dressed in red and scarlet of all sorts and contentions of shade?

The same liking for vivid contrast may be found in the folk-tales of Ireland. There it is the *red* Danes or Norsemen who persist in myth; and it is the red coat, not the khaki of the English soldiery, which figures in the evergreen memories of the Irish country people. I think of a story I heard from an old man in Bantry—of how, a century and a half ago, an invading French squadron sailed into the bay and the women of Bantry crowded

* F. R. Higgins, *The Gap of Brightness*. Macmillan & Co. Ltd.

9

out of their cottages to gaze at the surprising sight. But the Frenchmen mistook the red petticoats of the women for the red coats of the English and "by the Holy Man, their ships turned tail and away". So gratified was the English landlord that, for years after, he presented the tenantry of Bantry with an annual gift of red flannel.

Yes, it is the colourful detail that lives long in the historical imagination of Ireland.

"Why?" asked the poet Yeats, "why do people think of eternity as a long, long thing? It is the flash of light on a beetle's wing." And why must people think of colour in terms of great panoramic sweeps and brilliantly drawn-out seasons? It is in the small momentary contrasts: a deceptively sunny morning in March with snow on the ground, and the golden-brown bees emerging from the cherry tree and clustering sleepily on the snow-drops: or an Ulster garden in June suddenly sugared with hailstones that strike a million puffs of smoke from the heavily pollened yew trees: a yellow fire burning on green grass, the golden flutings of water on the Liffey, or the pink and green light of an Armagh apple orchard in blossom.

It is all these that make the colour of Ireland. Colour, as every poet who loves simile knows, cannot be likened to anything else; it is a thing in itself, stilled and static. It is only the contrasting play of light and shadow on a colour that makes it mobile and describable in terms of like-ness and metaphor, for words are made for movement and change. "Wouldn't you think?" said a Wicklow farmer, looking fondly at a beautifully marked red-and-white heifer, "wouldn't you think that the shadows of the clouds were passing over her back?"

Soft Atlantic rains that swathe and swaddle the Irish countryside give added depth and luminosity to its colours, like the brilliance of wet sea-pebbles. The low grey ceiling of cloud, endlessly opening and shutting, far from being monotonous, makes the land seem lighter and louder than the sky. Nowhere is grass so green, or, in parts, so lush: throw down your stick of an evening in a meadow in Meath and in the morning you will not be able to find it. Nowhere are the blues and purples of the hills so various and elusive, or the greys of the sky so softly tinged. A Viennese friend pointed out to me a subtle blueness in the Irish sky which he called "Irish blue" since he had seen it nowhere else. Moreover, in matters of cloud-colour there may even be parochial variations. Some years ago a visiting poet wrote an article for a Northern Ireland editor in which he praised the colour of the Irish sky. The editor blue-pencilled the phrase "Irish sky", changing it to "Ulster sky". Some may see in this action a certain political significance. But I prefer to think of it as part and parcel of that power of intense observation such as enables the West of Ireland fisherman to name and claim the very waves of the sea as his own.

II The Atlantic Fringe

IT is, of course, the Western Islanders who have the gayest sense of colour; in particular the people of the Aran Islands. Here where the thundering Atlantic pitches its lightning tents on the rocks, and the last waves rise up like swallows into the lofts of air—here, on this stony fender of Europe lives a community of two thousand people, a nest of Gaelic life. Aran is only thirty miles from Galway, but in its way of life it is hundreds of years from Europe.

At first sight, from the sea, you would think that no people could live on these islands—stone, stone everywhere with hardly enough grass to make a nose-bag for a beast. Soil is so scarce that in Aran, they say smilingly, the dead are buried standing up, in order to save ground. "Haven't they got all God's walls round them?" said the captain of our vessel as we approached Inishmore, the big Island. They certainly have. I never saw such stone walls. Strings and strings of them curling and coiling all over the place. Indeed it looks as if giant knitting-needles had knitted the walls and every stitch were a stone. Inside the deep walls nestle the greenest of tiny green fields—"gardens" they call them. They represent the blood and sweat of countless generations. Every foot of soil has been carried there on the backs of man and beast; baskets of earth taken from the sea-shore and spread out like a thick blanket on the rock. For all this green land is "made" land, hand-made. It is, as Robert Flaherty, who filmed it, declared, one of the wonders of the world and one of the great achievements of the human spirit. Against the grinding sea and grudging stone the islanders stand out as the most vivid and dignified community of the Western world.

I first saw the surprising scene on a day in May, with the white-haired Atlantic rollers rushing at express speed along the top of Inishmore, and the black beetle-like curraghs—tarred, canvas canoes—racing out to meet the ship as we anchored off Inishmaan. The colour was startling. Over the forehead of the white limestone island was drawn an ice-blue bandage of sky. Across the rocks a close procession filed down to the yellow strand, headed by a woman in crimson; behind her a score of red cattle; then came the body of islandmen in grey frieze cloth, and lastly the islandwomen, all in crimson.

The scene had a ritual air about it, for it was on this arranged day that the island cattle were to be swum out to the ship which would carry them to Galway Fair. On the sunlit beach the vivid groups of women and girls, shyly melting away before the camera like shadows before the sun, looked like graceful Victorians in their lovely crimson blouses and ankle-long petticoats and gay woven shawls.

Children in long red dresses and white pinafores, boys in cream jerseys, men in indigo-and-grey wrestling waist-deep in water with the despairing beasts as they urged them into the sea, the green and purple waves breaking in thin flashes of rainbow spray—all this was enough to make a man's mouth fall open and stay open. It is as if the very barrenness of that spartan environment calls forth a compensating prodigality of colour in the people. Looking from the lighthouse on the South Island one would see only a grey landscape of stone with maybe two red dots, followed by a darker dot, moving across it—two girls followed by a boy; for a girl here never goes courting alone with a lad. Red was always the traditional colour for an Aran woman, and when a girl married she would put on the red shawl. But except for the *crioss*, a plaited multicoloured belt, the island man's grey habit has the protective colouring of his stony surroundings. He is born not with a silver spoon in his mouth but with a stone in his fist. So he never bothers to open or build a gateway into a field: he simply knocks a gap in the wall and builds it up behind him. As one can see from the cliff-fortress of Dun Aengus—"in its setting the most magnificent barbaric monument in Europe"—his tradition of wall-building goes back to prehistoric days. He will even build a stone hut merely to get the rain-water from its roof. For wells are scarce here, though water is plentiful enough when the storm lifts the skirts of the Atlantic far above the head of the three-hundred-foot cliffs; for a moment the waves hang motionless in air, then slowly bend over and float away like grey ghosts across the face of the island.

III West Country

THE coastal reaches of the Connemara mainland are hardly less stony and waterless. Cromwell, who in his time restored so many churches to their pristine bareness, had his thunder stolen by the splendid grey barrenness of this limestone country. "There is not", complained one of his generals, "enough timber to hang a man, enough water to drown him, or enough earth to bury him." Indeed, I have heard of a girl from Erris, a bare part of Mayo, who on a journey to Castlebar saw a tree for the first time and promptly fainted, thinking it a giant of some sort. But in all this region no part is so startlingly naked as The Burren in North Clare, a series of low grey hills that look like the leavings of Creation, graceless and grassless and worn to the bone. Yet here is one of the wonders of Ireland for colour: fern, orchid, minute flowers, alpines of all colours and varieties flourish in the fissures and crevices, like scattered crumbs of ice and fire; a botanist's paradise.

There is truth, says the proverb, in a little cup. And there is intoxication even in a little grass or a tiny flower when found in a stony place. Contrast is all, in these matters. The most vivid colour I can remember was in that strange region approaching Carna, in Galway, a grey lunar landscape of frozen stone, relieved only by a white cottage with an apron of brilliant green in front of the door where water had been flung out, or an occasional wild gleam of montbretia among the rocks. "*Land,* is it?" said the Connemara peasant who was asked about the value of his holding. "When the cuckoo flies over my poor barren bit of land it isn't 'cuckoo!' he cries, but 'ha-ha!'" Yet it is precisely in such places where the land is lean and niggardly that man's imagination seems to blossom most. The bleak peninsula of Carna is one of the finest store-houses of Gaelic folk-tale and song, rich and vivid as the Edwardian-looking blouses and the long red skirts, with black velvet bands, worn by the women there. Landscape and people are indivisible.

"Cold Clare rock, and Galway rock and thorn" have always cried out for contrast, and for reinforcement against the grey dripping Atlantic mists that dowse the colours of hill, bog, loch and glen. But, of course, Ireland has her dry and brilliant times, and I am told that light on Achill Island has an actinic value as high as that of Mexico.

> *If I were a dog of sunlight I would bound*
> *From Phoenix Park to Achill Sound.*

"Oh!" exclaimed George Moore the novelist, as the train to Dublin carried him past a particularly lovely landscape in Connemara, "I would give ten pounds just to hold that view for five minutes!" "That's easily fixed," said his friend Oliver Gogarty, pulling the communication cord. "This will cost you only five pounds."

IV Urban East

TO leave the stony fastnesses of the West and to drive down through the slow, fat lands and torpid towns of the central plain is to feel that something of brightness has fallen from the air. Sharpness is gone; centuries have passed. Here in the Midlands all is leafy and lazy and green. The broad farms spread out richly on every side, and the great houses are far apart and lonely, like the farmers. How different from the pinched hill-sides of West Connaught and Donegal where the convivial cottages are as close as pins in the lapel of a coat, and the people are clustered like bees in hives of conversation. But to go west is not the answer to the townsman's problems. Dublin, at the other and urban end of the scale, has her own clear dyed-in-the-wool colour and character. On a glittering evening you may gaze from O'Connell's Bridge at the lingering sweep of old pastel-coloured buildings beside the Liffey, stretching into the distance as if into history. Or you may stand, of a clear morning, in Merrion Square and look up Fitzwilliam Street to the green hills beyond: here is the longest intact Georgian street to be found anywhere; half a mile of it. These grave rust-red Augustan buildings with their elegant painted doors and delicate fanlights once housed the vanishing cream of Dublin Society, and still they have a vastly leisured air about them as if the front-door bell-pulls that were plucked a century and a half ago were only now beginning to tinkle in some far back passage. In summer, bright striped cloths cover the doors, gaily coloured as the noses of the hard-drinking country gentlemen who come to town for Horse Show week. But the best vintage or vantage point for colour in this city is an upper room in the General Post Office from which to look down on the fruit-market in Moore Street with its peacock-hued display and its voluble crowd of Dublin characters. Go into one of the dark inkwell pubs there and treat yourself to a pint of porter while you listen to their talk. If you are lucky you may overhear one of those incomparable Dublin remarks that throw a shadow of silence on the company. "Luck, is it?" says one man. "Sure I've never any luck at all. If a mermaid was cut in two I'd be sure to get the fishy half." Colour, in Ireland, is seldom put on canvas; it goes into the talk, and I can imagine no greyer fate than to be a deaf man in Dublin. The vivid phrase, the witty remark, the oratorical and florid turn of speech are always on the tip of the tongue of the man in the street.

In strongest contrast to the demotic colour of Moore Street and working-class Dublin I would choose the charming little Casino at Marino, a jewel of eighteenth-century hieratic architecture built for Lord Charlemont by Sir William Chambers. In its dingy setting of barbed wire it looks sadly out of place today, but no setting can efface the pleasure of its perfect classical proportions, its lovely zodiac ceiling, its gilts and blues and terracottas that breathe an alien and Mediterranean air.

Still, Ireland's most colourful exports are her talkers and her most valuable imports are her listeners; and up to now she has always been able to show a credit balance. Of all Irish cities, Dublin, in my opinion has the most industrious talkers. James Joyce who immortalised them in his novel *Ulysses*, was aggrieved when a Soviet critic denounced his book as "capitalist". "There are", said Joyce to a friend, "no wealthy characters

14

in my book." "Ah," said the friend, "but there are no workers in it either." No, just lovely industrious talkers, coiling and intercoiling like eels in wordy wedlock, reminding one of the illuminated monkish manuscript, the *Book of Kells* ("the most beautiful book in the world") with its free-flowing Celtic line endlessly and wonderfully interlaced. "If talk were cloth"—as they say in Ireland—"a man might have the makings of an overcoat." And a waterproof one at that, I would add, for the best talking-shop in Ireland is the pub, "the layman's monastery". Externally, the pub may be garishly painted; but within, the colours are usually dark and sober, as fits the solemn business of drinking. There are no bright distractions to compete with the conversation. "Even the drinks", as one Dubliner remarked, "are funereal." Pints of frothing porter—the dark wine of the Liffey—line the counter, "the brown lace sinking in the empty glass". Indeed I have known a pub on the Quays where the washing-up woman could tell the fortunes of the customers by looking at the rings in their glasses. The most fortunate people, of course, drink whisky, though even here they will wantonly prefer a drop of good poteen—which is colourless—to the golden drop of bonded or "parliament" whisky. Colourlessness is not a sign of weakness. "Gently dip, but not too deep." Years ago, when Mr. Arthur Balfour visited the West of Ireland he was fêted by a body of Clifden citizens who sought to influence him in the matter of a railway that was to be built there. At dinner, he drank knowledgeably from the decanter of colourless poteen provided, liberally diluting it from a neighbouring decanter of water. Unfortunately, both decanters were of poteen, and the potent upshot and hangover of it all was that the railway liverishly refused to go where it was wanted. Most Irish whiskeys are pot-distilled, but the patent still, used by Scottish distillers, was invented by Aeneas Coffee of Dublin in the early 1820's. Several years later, Thwaites, a Dubliner, invented soda water.

One habit, which I cannot but deplore, sins against the original righteousness of Irish colourlessness in drink. Throughout the Midlands, in Dublin City itself, and on the long road from Dublin through Mitchellstown to Cork, one may find men drinking a curious muddy-red beverage: it consists of English beer with a dollop of raspberry cordial in it as a sweetener, invented, no doubt, as a sort of shandy by a backsliding cockney convert to the faith of Father Matthew, the famous Cork teetotaller. The normal Irishman sticks to extremes, to the opaquity of porter or the candour of whisky. He will drink tea, of course, in prodigious quantities, but it must be strong enough for a mouse to trot on it, and the worst word that a Wexford man has for weak-coloured tea is to say that "you could spear a shark through forty fathoms of it."

15

V Southern Retrospect

TO go from Dublin to Cork is to cross the Curragh, the great open grassy plain that is heaven and headquarters for race horses. Not even the famous "Blue Grass" region of Kentucky can better these limestone pastures which give bone to beast and bring wealth to Kildare. Kildare is the typically flat midland county of wide silences and subdued tones. Long canals stretch across it like strips of linen. Cool white cloud, warm mulberry-coloured bog, depths of bright green sphagnum, brilliant dragonfly, nodding miles of dancing bog-cotton and lazy sedges give the country a far-away and long-ago look; and everywhere

The wrestling curlew in the bog
Argues with a curving sound.

By contrast—though not by distance—it's a long way to Tipperary with its fat valley land—the "Golden Vein" of Ireland—its background of blue mountains and green glens, gapped by yellow sky, and, centering all, the high limestone Rock of Cashel topping the plain, as if on stilts. On this Rock the kings of Munster held footing for centuries, and here are the remains of Cormac's Chapel (the best example of Irish Romanesque), a round tower, an ancient cross, a castle, a roofless mediaeval cathedral and —below the Rock—a ruined abbey.

"Ireland", wrote Kohl, a nineteenth-century traveller, "is the first country in Europe for ruins." Few buildings have had long standing in this up-and-down land, and one fact neatly points the troubled course of Irish history—that whereas England today has some 10,000 parish churches whose services have gone on unbrokenly from the Middle Ages and whose roofs have never been removed, Ireland has but five such churches. The trouble, of course, has been her visitors, and the successive waves of invasion and rebellion that swept the country. Everywhere the grey reminders and ivied remains of history stipple the Irish landscape; the slender round tower with conical cap, used against the Dane; the thick-skinned Norman castle with its bullnecked keep; the stand-offish Elizabethan castle with its hedgehog battlements; the Big House so liberally fortified once with food and drink, reflecting the peace of the Augustan ascendency, but now deserted and roofless.

Yet the paucity of fine preserved building is partly due to a native intransigence. England has taken pride in her ancient buildings. Ireland has been prodigally careless in the matter, being more interested in people than in places; it is enough, she feels, to have history in her bones and on her tongue rather than in her possessions.

Not that Ireland is lacking in notable houses. Caledon, in County

Tyrone, and Russborough House in Wicklow, are Augustan examples that could hardly be bettered: but these and their like were built in Georgian days, in the heyday of Anglo-Irish society and power when the absentee-total landlords came home to roost and roister in Dublin for a time, and "the plentiful luxuries of the table, and rich furniture of the wine-cellar were never surpassed, if equalled, among the gentry of any country." "You are not", confided Mrs. Delany to a friend in England, "invited to any private gentleman of a thousand a year or less that does not give you seven dishes at one course, and Burgundy and Champagne." With all this went—or rather came—a flowering of the art of architecture and plasterwork in Dublin, and the crafts of silver, glass and furniture making. For it is the wealth and leisure of urban life that make possible a material expansion of the arts. A rural and scattered society has neither means nor time for painting, sculpture or architecture. Ireland today has her good painters, sculptors and architects, but in the past she had perforce to put her considerable powers into the colourful and oral forms of folk-song and storytelling so that nowhere in Europe now are there more considerable remnants of these, and no rural people has a readier tongue or a finer fancy.

VI The Far-off Hills

IT is only among the Gaelic-speaking folk of the south-west, west and north-west that the storyteller or *seanchai* still practises his immemorial art. For life in those parts is remote from cities: the farmer's or fisherman's farthest excursion is to the nearest market. "And tell me, Sergeant Clever," remarked one young Kerryman, "if you had no picture-house, no playhouse, and no cunning versatile radio at the tips of your fingers, no amusement whatsoever from head to head of the week except what was painted on the square above a cottage half-door (the highest excitement being the coming and going of cloud-caps on a mountain) wouldn't you, too, be hungry for the lovely dovetailed talk?" Talk that intoxicates and that colours their grey existence by its grandeur. When the day's dusty duty has been done, the last boat drawn up on the strand, and the mountain sides and sea lochs that fringe the Western ocean are dark, then in some whitewashed kitchen in a glen, where the turf-fire glows like a berry and the cricket—"the cock of the ashes"—wakens, the tangle of Gaelic voices singles out as the Storyteller spreads his fingers for attention and begins his tale. Maybe it is a wonder-tale about kings and queens, a tale that crossed the roads of Europe from the East a thousand years ago, passing from mouth to mouth till it came to rest in this silence beside the Atlantic. And the *seanchaí* tells it with great play of hands and traditional phrase: "He was catching up on the March wind that was ahead of him, and the March wind that was behind him could not catch up on him. Until it was high noon, until the bright lights of day were going from him, the darkness of night drawing near him, the white horse going in the shadow of the dockleaf, if the dockleaf waited even an inch for him. . . ."

But the art of storytelling is vanishing. "Few revolutions", says W. P. Kerr, "or general changes of habit have been more important than that which cut off the old romantic popular traditions of folk-lore and ballads in the nineteenth century and put modern educational text books in their place. This means a change in the mind of modern civilised human beings, making them unlike all their ancestors. They learn nothing now in the way that all generations learned their ballads and fairy stories. These things may come to them by way of books. They do not come as part of their real life from the mouth of their nurse and grandmother."

Also, with the passing of that world there passes a strange colourful wonderland inhabited by giants, dragons, monsters and fairies which the modern mind can never know as they were once known. For these things were not invented to please a childish mind or pass an idle hour. They were precisely seen and believed in, in all their shapes and colours. I can recall, in springtime, sitting by a turf-fire within sound of the western sea, and listening to an old man telling, with every vivid sign of conviction and memory, an adventure that happened to him—"One evening", he said, "in the autumn, I was going along the road into a lonely glen. I had a basket on my shoulder, and I had a can, too. I heard the noise inside the cliff, and I made out as closely as I could that it was a churn—a churning vessel, at work. I stopped and was listening to it for a while. Then he—for it was a fairy in the cliff—took his hammer and started striking a nail, and I said to myself that it was a shoe he was putting on his horse. 'Well,' says I, 'this isn't a good place for me to be!' I went off along the road a good piece and looked around me again towards the same place, and there was a nice small man out on the road, and a white horse by him, as white as the snow. His own clothes were as white as the snow, like the suit of a baker exactly. He had a small red cap, with some kind of a small stripe in the middle. I started to look at him, and it seemed very strange to me the likes of him to be there. He was looking at me, and he holding the horse's head, and then he began to beckon to me, and did it three times. 'Oh,' says I to myself, 'I'd better run home as fast as I can.' I made off along the road. I was wearing a small round cap with a tassel in the middle of it on top, but I didn't know at the time, with the excitement, whether I'd a cap on me at all. On I went, and on. I wasn't running, but indeed if I

18

wasn't I was walking as fast in Ireland as I could. Oh, he was forcing the little horse up on my heels! I used to pull into the fence, to give him room to pass on the road, but 'twas no use. He was urging on his horse all the time, you'd think she'd strike her two legs on my heels! That went on and there was sweat falling from me. There was sweat falling from my nose down on the ground with fear. In one way there was no fear in me, but still there must have been, till I came to a house that was west there. The light was lit in it—Ned Pole's that's there now. The light was lit in it. I came in front of the gate, and that's when my man, the fairy, stopped. I came home, and I assure you that I didn't leave anything in my bowels that I didn't put out, with fright. I fell into the house backwards."

Here is a last colourful remnant from a long-ago world, a world in which the storytellers were the living libraries of Europe—a Europe which had no books, no newspaper, no cinema, a Europe whose only entertainment was the winter's tale told by a passing traveller. "It used to be", said a West Cork schoolmaster to me, "that there was one particular house in our neighbourhood for storytelling, and my father took me every second night. I was fifteen at the time, and, whether in Gaelic or English, I'd be delighted with the fairy stories. Going home at night, if a widowed leaf dropped from a holly bush I'd leap a foot." But the radio has taken away the audience of the storyteller just as the printed page has taken away his memory; and the pictures that were once seen in a turf-fire are now seen only in glorious technicolour. In Listowel, a little town in Kerry, a friend took me one night to meet an old storyteller, the only man left, he said, who could tell "The King of Ireland's Son" in the traditional grand manner; but I never saw the old man for we found he had gone to his enemy's house—the Cinema.

It was in a Listowel pub (with a wonderful coloured plaster figure over the door) that I listened to a travelling umbrella-mender comparing notes with a tinker, talking about the place in Clare where a beggar would be given a beaten-up egg; or the village in Kerry where you would be invited to have a ninth cup of tea; or Kinvarra in Galway—"a good place for a poor man. By the saints, they'll open the door to you. But Limerick! you'd have to take the shady side of the road there!"

Always it's in the lonely parts of the country that people are warmest and most hospitable, being hungry for the talk and the stories that the stranger brings with him. Imagination feeds on lack. It is in the grey west, for example, that people, looking out to sea, have sometimes glimpsed, humped on the horizon, the fabulous island of Hy Brasil, the lost Atlantis, green and golden, and glittering with snow-white houses and immortal fruit: if only, says tradition, a fisherman were to put a burning lump of turf or coal on that island, it would remain for ever his, instead of

19

sinking again below the waves. For the far-off hills of the imagination are green, but cold; only the fire and warmth of the human spirit can redeem and preserve them. All over Ireland, in country places, one finds that the kitchen hearth is looked on as the heart of the matter; if the fire is allowed to go out, then the luck or life of the house goes with it. I have always felt that something of this ancient belief persists in the townsman's habit of lighting a fire in a sick-room. Certainly there are many farmhouses in Ireland where the fire has not gone out for generations: each night the ashes are carefully raked over the embers to preserve them till morning, occasionally with a prayer, such as the one I have heard an old woman in the Gaeltacht say: "I preserve the fire as Christ preserves all. Brigid at the two ends of the house, and Jesus in the centre. The three angels and the three apostles who are highest in the Kingdom of Grace, guarding this house and its contents until day." Prayer and peat, countrywise, go together, whereas the coal fire and the oil-burning radiator do not urbanely lend themselves to piety.

VII South-West

"HEAVEN", remarked an old Kerry woman to a friend of mine, "lies in the south-west, a foot and a half above the height of a man." I have never been able to make out the meaning of that meticulous statement but I would agree that Killarney is nearer to heaven than most places. With its looking-glass lakes—"heaven's reflex"—and its mountains flowing down in a riot of corrugated draperies, it is unwearyingly lovely and lonely and unspoilable.

Rain or shine (and I have enjoyed weeks of wonderful weather on end in the south and west) there are few landscapes whose colour, scale and contrast impress so immediately; whether on a gloomy evening crossing the Conor Pass through the sombre blue-black mountains with their silver leakage of lakes and their immense umber bosses and bases of bog; or, on a sunny morning, following the daft corkscrew road over the Healy Pass, the sky at one's feet and the world at one's head; here and there a bright breast of grass, or a warm armpit of turf, or a watching eye of water, shows below. Little three-cornered fields like bright green handkerchiefs hang to the rocks, with black Kerry cows looking as toylike as the mountainy fields they graze on, and stepping so delicately that they wouldn't even jar on a schoolmaster who had a hangover. In the sheltered ruts of the valleys, and along the peninsulas and silver inlets of Kerry and Cork, the most notable colour is the red-and-purple of the fuchsia. It will cling closely to a wall, winding through the dry stone interstices like a minute-leafed creeper, or it will spread itself prodigally in tall hedges and trees with warm golden branches as thick as a man's arm. The hugged mild climate suits it perfectly, as it does the arbutus and the thickets of rhododendron.

More than anything else, a white-washed wall overhung with blood-red drops of fuchsia recalls the Irish scene for me: an afternoon spent lying on the cliffs, looking out at the Blasket Islands (the next parish to America), the gannets flashing like bits of mirror, the red-legged choughs busy in the cliffs, and the black tarred canoe with a holy medal at its prow dancing across the waves below. Or a morning with a gamekeeper, in a mountain-glen cottage above Cahirciveen, and himself pointing out the place where Finn McCoul's hound had leaped those very hills two thousand years ago in pursuit of a deer, or where gold had once been seen in the depths of the nearby lake, and ditches had been dug to drain the lake (for the Irish countryman is a dyed-in-the-wool, dried-in-the-bog realist) but in the morning the ditches were full of blood.

In the whole ring of the south-west, however, there is nothing to match the colour and spectacle of Puck Fair, in Killorglin. Here, on 10th August, Puck, a great buck goat from the mountains is crowned king, and for three days, from his fifty-foot throne of scaffolding, he lords it over the unsleeping town. And night and day an endless family of farmers moves in its thousands through the shops and pubs below, as if through a house of many rooms, drinking in enough talk and palaver to do them for the rest of the year. From all over Ireland, the tinkers, beggars, ballad-singers, horse-dealers, sleight-of-hand men converge. The road leading to the town is lined with the tinkers' round-hooded caravans, brightly painted in reds and yellows, and all-glorious-within with gleaming brass and mirror and gayest chintz and chinaware. Hedges suddenly sprout a thousand coloured clouts of washing. Then, on Gathering Day, the first day of the Fair, the cattle-thronged street leading up to the scaffold is crammed crimson with people from all arts and parts. There are sightseers on the chimney-pots as the coronation procession comes into the square, headed by outriders in vivid sashes and followed by pipers in saffron and green. A piercing whistle clears the way for Puck himself, swathed in royal purple, mounted on a green pedestal on an outrageously red motor lorry. At the bottom of the scaffold a girl, silver crowned, places a golden crown on the splendid horned head, the pipers strike up, the people roar, and King Puck, with glaring yellow eye, ascends by block pulley and rope to the seventh heaven of his sovereignty. And an old tinker woman, gazing triumphantly after him, shouts defiantly at the crowd—"A Coffee was the first man to put up The Puck!" For the Coffees are one of the old tinker tribes. This is Ireland *en fête* and at its best, with the pints of stout loosening the talking-tapes of men's tongues, loosening the purse-strings of strong-fisted farmers, loosening the fiddler's fingers and the dancers' feet and the year-long loneliness of closed-up glensfolk, and always with the traditional ease and dignity that enlarges everybody. "We have no trouble," said the Guarda Superintendent to me, "for the pubs and the shops are open all night. If they weren't we *would* have trouble." In the small dark hours of the morning to walk and talk freely in a wide-awake town is itself a breathing wonder to people, and a strangely liberating one. "Ah," said a cattle-dealer to me, "you should have been at Ballinasloe when the tinkers kinged young Ward. That was a day! The old king, his father, had just died." "A tinker", he went on, "can spoil the sale of a beast if he's not allowed in on it. By right and usage he's supposed to have a hand in the sale of any animal at any fair in Ireland."

VIII The Town

WINTER or Summer, North or South, the monthly Fair Day in a market town is, by immemorial custom, the high day for colour and clash of talk, and commerce. All over Ireland there are "towns" so small that you would only have to put your foot out to be in the country; towns so deeply ingrown and quiet that there is nothing to be seen all week but the bicycle leaning against a wall or a shopkeeper looking into his own window; a spiral of rooks settling like tea-leaves into the trees; or an idler leaning over a bridge waiting for the water to stop. But suddenly on a Fair Day it changes and the town jumps to attention. For this is the day for the shuttlecock game of buying and selling, with one man crowing and crowding it over another man in the market place. From the first bloodshot blink of dawn the roads are filled with a raindrop pattering of hooves. Maybe a grey muslin of rain, like a mist, hangs overhead, and the streets are jammed with muddy men and wet, steaming cattle; with the traffic of cars trickling and treacling round them. No one moves aside for the cars, for there were markets in these places before there were motor roads to them, and the memory of that is in every man's bones. Here is colour galore. Big red bullocks with a soft fur of rain on them and thistles of smoke coming out of their noses. Biscuit-coloured Jerseys, splotchy bulls, black Kerrys, white cows (whose lack of colour is traditionally disliked), blue cows which are popular, and which are got (as the Greeks got their classic blue vases) by covering a black with a white. Strings of horses—"a white horse was ever and always kept for weddings and for Sundays"—and perhaps a piebald or "batty" pony, so-called from Beatty's Circus which used to tour Ireland. Now and again one sees a cow with a bit of red rag tied to her tail in order to avert the evil eye. All day long, men and beasts stand impassively in the rain, as idle as a piper's little finger. You would think nobody meant to buy or sell at all, yet everyone is watchful. Of a sudden, an excited crowd gathers round a beast, wrinkling and wrangling like a knot of maggots. In the middle of them, with faces solemn and stiff as grave-diggers, two men face each other. One owns the beast, the other bids for it. It's a battle of wits and will-power now, and dignity demands that neither man should publicly bat an eyelid or budge an inch on his price. But the "tangler" or middleman is there, traditionally ready to bridge the gulf and split the difference between them and save face for them, and to get them to strike hands together in token of compromise. For his services he gets a rake-off. But it isn't really the money that matters. It isn't even the beast that matters; it's the men behind it and the delightful battle of wits and words that it involves, and the cockcrow of triumph at getting the better of the other man. "I thought you told me", says a buyer, looking scornfully at a cow, "that this beast had no fault. And yet she's blind of an eye!" "That", says the seller quietly, "isn't her fault. That's her misfortune." And at the end of the day he goes home leaping like a dog with two tails to recount his bit of repartee.

Everything, except the cat, is bought and sold at the Fair. "A penny for the ticket, and sixpence for the Prize," shouts the lottery man. "The greatest jewel in the world. As Euclid, the great Egyptian philosopher, says. . . ."

"Come on, now," cries the old clothes vendor holding up a red coat to a shy young farmer, "*there's* a coat for you! Try it on your back and you'll be head porter before half an hour!"—"Look, lady, a fine pair of trousers! The mother and father of all trousers. You'll never have to soap your son's legs to slide him into *this* pair. Hold them, lady," he says, handing her a pair of purple corduroys. "They won't take a bite out of you. One pound, I say! Fifteen shillings! Ten shillings! A crown, then! Trousers are coming down. Don't be alarmed, lady. . . ."

And so the patter runs on till nightfall. Talk, talk, talk. Nobody cares overmuch about the issue. What matters is the artful word, the cut and thrust of wit, the war of wills. Here, for a day, the great colourful drama of life is played out on the stage of a little town, and, for the Irish countryman, the fair has therefore all the clash and clang of the world.

As night falls, the pubs fill with gossip and story and folk-song. "It was this kind of story exactly", I heard a man say one evening at the end of a long tale, "that Dante listened to and learned from." "Do you tell me that!" exclaimed his companion, "there's a cartload of meaning in that story!" And, on another such evening, I happened on a lad who was playing on an ivy leaf (as on a mouth organ), making a high-pitched strident music, quick and spirited. Half a century ago this was not an uncommon accomplishment: in the town of Castlebar, within living memory, there was a band composed of ivy-leaf players. "For the purpose of playing", explained the lad in the pub to me, "you must choose a green leaf that has been picked in the shadow of an early morning. If the sun comes at it the leaf is too strong. You want a weak leaf for this job. By preference, one that has been picked in the fall, between October and March." He himself must have picked his leaves in the blue blaze of June, for he kept dipping them into his pint of stout, in order to wet and weaken them.

IX The Townland

FROM Bantry Bay to Derry Quay the distinctive feature of the small Irish town is its long straggling main street.

> *Long hungry Cookstown,*
> *Where the dogs are loose and the stones tied down.*

quipped a beggar who had tramped its one-and-a-quarter-mile length to no purpose.

Gay Georgian house, Victorian shopfront, colour-washed cottage, stand end to end along the highway, as if on convoy; as if indeed, they had merely halted there on the way to some far-off forgotten event. There is no feeling of settlement such as one gets in an English town with its centrifugal pattern of church, inns and shops. Perhaps it is part of the mobility of the Irish character. ("If you want to hold an old position," said a Korean War-correspondent to me, "put in an English regiment. If you want to take a new position, put in an Irish regiment. That's how I see it.") But more surely it indicates a different social history. The old Gaelic order was essentially rural in character. It produced no large cities and towns of its own. Dublin, Limerick, Wexford and Waterford, were Norse foundations, as the Irish word for "market" was a Norse introduction. Derry and Belfast were planted by English settlers. Even the village, as a nodal point in rural life, was foreign to the Celt. His society was hierarchical in structure (the parish priest is now the last exemplar of that); his tribe was the family, in all its degrees of kinship; and the family territory was the "townland" with its beehive cluster of convivial houses such as one still sees in the west and north-west fringe. And still, today, family loyalties play an astonishingly large part in the shaping of public life in Ireland, and urban outlooks there are tinged by rural attitudes to a degree not obtaining in industrialised Britain.

Anyone who has lived long enough in the Irish countryside will have sensed how one townland of people differs from another townland in the minutiae of its manners, character, dress, custom, taboo, almost as if each had inherited a hidden family tradition which colours all it touches. "The townlands in turn group themselves into baronies corresponding to the petty kingdoms of old. Writers tell us that even into the nineteenth century one barony could be easily distinguished from another by the dresses peculiar to each. Thus there were the dark blue and damson of Cork and Waterford, the grey of Kerry and the blue of Galway."

If we move to the still larger field of the provinces, and, beyond that to the political grouping of Ireland today into North and South it becomes clearer that colour in the Emerald Isle goes hand in hand with contrast. To talk about the Irish scene without noting the considerable symbolism of Orange and Green would be to blind oneself to the character and history of the country for the last century and a half.

X The Orange North

Then heigho the lily-o,
The royal loyal lily-o,
Beneath the sky, what flower can vie
With Ireland's Orange Lily-o?
There's not a flower in Erin's bower
Can match the Orange Lily-o.

Throughout the "Orange North" you will recognise a Protestant garden by the presence of the Orange Lily. The sight of the tell-tale flower, signalising the victory of the Protestant William of Orange over the Catholic King James in 1690, recalls many a hot sultry "Twelfth of July" in Ulster, with the red bonfires ringworming the streets at night, the windows glaring like bloodshot eyes, the brass door-knockers glowing like red noses, the brave house gables painted with pictures of King Billy crossing the Boyne on his white horse, and the walls of the town trembling with the heavy curtains of the continual drumming. Colour, as folk emblem, is not a fortuitous thing. The Orange Lily seems to me to represent very well the close, sultry, emotional character of the Ulsterman, just as the white and green Easter Lily—symbol of resurgence—has in it the clear, cold air of hope that always inspired Nationalist Ireland. The two characters, however much opposed, are complementary.

> *The same good soil sustaining both,*
> *Makes both united flourish,*
> *But cannot give the Orange growth*
> *And cease the Green to nourish.*

"If there wasn't the one sort," as we say in Ireland, "there wouldn't be the other." To lose either opponent would be to lose the whole tang and tension of life. "God is good," remarked an old Ulster roadmender to a friend of mine, "and the devil isn't bad, thank God." The Irish mind has always had a liking for drama and a fond eye for the oppositions of things, and it is this which lends such friction and fire to its politics. By comparison, other countries seem grey and tame and toothless after the clash and colour of the Irish scene.

What spectacle in Ireland is more lively or colourful than that of The Twelfth of July, when the Northern towns are airy with rainbow bunting, and day-long processions of dignified Ulstermen in bowler hats, navy-blue suits and orange sashes march to "the Field", headed by flute and drum bands. Above them float the gayest silken banners that belly out like flames, red, blue, black, yellow and green, depicting the gravest of subjects: Adam and Eve in the Garden; The Siege of Derry; Johnston of Bally-kilbeg; Gideon Drinking From the Brook; The Secret of England's Greatness (Queen Victoria handing the Bible to a Black Man)—and—over and over again—a favourite bone of contention, David and Goliath. In front thunder the big painted drums, beaten by shirtsleeved Samsons till the blood runs down their wrists. It is all part of the serious drama of life, an outlet for religious and political feelings. To dramatise is to civilise; it is to work out one's salvation on a stage, and the Irishman has always preferred to work *out* his dilemma rather than to bleed inwardly with it. Conflict, friction, opposition, is the very stuff of drama: can we imagine an Oedipus Rex, a Hamlet, a St. Joan, without it?

My own favourite piece of folk-drama in Ulster is "The Sham Fight" at Scarva, on 13th July. There, on a field fronting the seventeenth-century manor house, the Battle of the Boyne is re-enacted each year before immense crowds of Ulstermen. William of Orange, plumed and sworded on a white horse, leads his colourful soldiers against King James, on a dark horse. They clash, and James falls, whereupon William gallantly descends and courteously raises him to his feet again, in order

26

no doubt that he may fight another day; for, as every Irishman knows, to liquidate an enemy is to remove the reason for one's own existence. "I pray God for my enemies," said A.E., that most lovable of Irish mystics, "but I pray God that I may *have* enemies to keep me alive." I am reminded by this of a certain bipartisan village in the North which boasted only one big drum, (an expensive item), the properly of the local Orange Lodge. However, in order to keep responsible belligerency alive, the drum was lent, on occasions, to the opposing band of Fenians. Moreover, the drum was painted with loyal Orange emblems for one half of its circumference, and with "rebel" emblems for the other. Here indeed was that unity in difference, that straightforward all-roundness of contraries which speaks for Ireland but which strangers find it hard to understand. Opposition is in the bones of the Irishman; it's in his breath. It may take the form of words, such as Joycean pun, Shavian paradox, Wilde-ish epigram, or plain Irish Bull. Or it may take the form of a drumming-match, in which two Ulstermen will stand up facing each other with their big red drums belly to belly, and proceed to beat out the same level rhythm together: until at last one of them through failure of will-power wavers and loses his beat, and instantly the other drummer's rhythm is on top of his, triumphant and trampling it down.

The Irish landscape may be misty, it may have its foggy dews and mysterious grey Celtic twilights, but there is nothing misty about the compensating Irish character. "Even farther from the truth is the idea that Celtic poetry is misty and loves subdued colours. On the contrary, its characteristic is sharp, clear outline, a cloudless atmosphere, a passion for bright, primary colours." In fact, the loudest and most opposed colours are the most loved, yet all will be made to blend as in the lovely colour-speckled homespun tweeds of the country. But blending is not blurring, and, whether in matters of dress or politics, the Irishman likes to keep his antagonisms sharp and clean, and to show his colours: he insists therefore on taking sides, and on knowing what side other people are on. He cannot understand a half-way attitude, an in-and-between tone. In the course of census-taking in Northern Ireland, a local policeman who had collected the return-forms had reason to call on an English colonel. "I'm sorry to be bothering you, sir," said he, producing the colonel's filled-in paper, "but it's about this class of a question here—Religion. You say you are an 'Agnostic'. Now would you mind making the answer a wee bit fuller? Could you say whether you are a Protestant agnostic or a Catholic agnostic?" No drab grey compromise, no cloud of unknowing, but an out-and-out, black or white statement is relished here.

XI Black and White

I HAVE often noticed that the contrast of black and white is one that appeals greatly to the Irish eye. One day a friend of mine was walking through that finest of Dublin squares, St. Stephen's Green, when he saw a stranger on his knees, in a shrubbery, acting in a curious manner. My friend, who has an inquiring mind, at once got upon his knees and followed the man through the gloomy green tunnels of the shrubbery. Suddenly, at the edge of a clearing, the stranger turned, put his finger to his lips for silence, and pointed ahead. There, on a green lawn, was a white blackbird, rampant. "Do you often do this?" whispered my friend to the stranger. "Oh yes," said he. "Whenever I hear of a white blackbird in Ireland I go to see it." I wonder would his interest have extended to the white magpie which I once saw in County Armagh. Perhaps it would have been exciting but upsetting to him, for the Irish countryman traditionally feels bound to placate the black-and-white magpie (if seen singly and not in a pair) by saying "Good morning, Mr. Magpie", and spitting. But how should one greet a white magpie? White, whether in bird or beast, has a mysterious and disturbing effect on the Irish countryman's mind. How strongly, for instance, the old beliefs concerning that royally white bird, the swan, persist in Ireland.

For the poet, the brilliant bird has always been a symbol of other-worldliness: and for the peasant it carries old far-off memories of that legendary Ireland in which the pagan King Lir's children were turned into swans, doomed to float round Ireland for lonely centuries till they heard the sound of a Christian bell.

I have known a young man in the West to shoot a swan and to ask his mother to prepare it for dinner. She did so, but nobody in the house would venture to eat it, and eventually it was buried, with shame and embarrassment.

Maybe it is the liking for strong black and white contrast that makes me partial to the Belfast I knew, with its long files of women and girls in black shawls, streaming out of the linen-mills; or the dark city at dusk with the rain stippling the puddles and silvering the pavements, and the "Islandmen" thronging the red tramcars and filling the red-blinded pubs. What drink then could be more proper than the white-headed pints of black porter? It was in Belfast too that I came across a dark and curious usage among house-painters. There I have seen them mix a bottle of stout into the paint in the belief that it fixed the colour better and gave it a lasting quality. So deeply ingrained was this belief that, employed on a job, they would go without their elevenses each morning in order to visit the nearest pub for a working supply.

By far the most contrary of landscapes in Ireland is to be found along the Antrim coast where the clear opposition of black basalt and white chalk cliff, broken only by the deep green pockets of the glens or a red sandstone bay, is unforgettably vivid; the sun squinting through fistfuls of cloud on lovely chequered headlands, on grey and yellow aprons of beach and green sea. Geologically, Ulster is the most varied part of these islands and in its small scope it has all the diversity of colour that goes with sudden contour changes, with lean mountain and fat lowland and middling hill.

"And where does *your* land lie?" a Slieve Gullion farmer was asked. "It doesn't lie," he replied. "It stands straight up with its backside to the mountain." The land lends its character and diversity to those who cultivate it. One is tempted to compare the quick, abrupt mountainy farmer with the slow-speaking methodical valley farmer who seems to have fields and fields in him, with every haycock a thought. But man, in turn, lends his colour to the land. How much of the mixed colour of Ulster is due to its patchwork farming, its multitude of small holdings and tiny fields that are graced, not just with a monotony of grass or oats, but with every possible crop, and traced with the lineaments of ancient history.

Earth wears the shapes of use in colour and curve.

The nodding field of blue-flowering flax, the bleaching green with its bright webs of linen, stem back to the little white-washed cottages that once housed a multitude of handlooms, and where men wove the stuff of poetry as well as linen. I have often noticed, in the west and south-west of Ireland, where the cottage loom may still be seen at work, that the weaver tends to be the philosopher of the community, and a radical-minded one at that. His careful, intricate handwork gives him much time for thinking. All the families for whom he weaves a web of cloth are mapped in his mind, with all their doings and idiosyncracies, and every farmer must at one time or another become his customer. So his house becomes a discussion centre for politics, religion, events, people, weather and work. Every subject from tiddleywinks to the Trinity is canvassed. I have listened, in a weaver's shed in the remote Aran Islands, to men discussing the comparative merits of the radio and the gramophone. In the end they agreed that the gramophone disc was the more wonderful invention, for it gave you the voices of *dead* men whereas the radio gives you only the voices of *living* men. To the Irish countryman the past is omnipresent, shaping and colouring the everyday stuff of his life.

So there is more in colour and shape than meets the eye. Those round, whitewashed pillars which form the gateways to the fields and farms of Down and Antrim may indicate a lack of indigenous wood. But more surely to me they are the instant and diminished reminders of the ancient monolith, twin pillars that guard the entrances and exits to life and death. Why else should they be massive, out of proportion to their purpose? And why, when a farmer builds a new farmhouse, does he carefully erect these pillars at the entrance to the "loanin" or long lane leading to his house, often without bothering ever to swing a gate on them? The hidden reasons that underlie Reason are always operative. Once I asked an Irish farmer as to what had happened to his little white dog. "Oh," he said, "it bit the postman and we had to destroy it. You can't have a dog going about biting people. It will get you into trouble." A rational enough statement; but it was only months later that I learned the deeper and older reason for its destruction, the sympathetic belief that, as the dog dies, the bite gets better. But you will notice that old dark superstition and the new bright rationalism have a common factor and result—the dog dies.

XII Contraries

EVERY colour in an Irish county has a story to it. Armagh with its orchards, outlined with delicate white plum blossom in April, and bosomed with pink apple blossom in May, bespeaks an English settlement, but its lime-washed eighteenth-century farmhouses, ochre and pink, and salmon, have the Irish habit. And Armagh City—the ecclesiastical capital of Ireland—with its *English Street* of grey elegant stone buildings, its *Scotch Street* of tall thrifty painted emporiums, its *Irish Street* of small, dark, intimate, intriguing shops (where blue spirits may not legally be sold) has all the national dyes clearly running together; the city is dominated by two cathedrals, Protestant and Catholic, perched on opposing hills "as if on the horns of a dilemma".

Among a people so given to dramatic oppositions one may expect to find strong and surprising contrast of all sorts. It may be the blue and orange of a country cart, or the red-oxide-painted doors of white-washed farm buildings. It may be a verse about falling snow, written by an Antrim schoolboy:

> *No rainbow now will yawn the sky,*
> *Nor the sun the windows burn;*
> *But the little puffs of wadding owl by,*
> *And people mouth their fists and mourn.*

Or it may be a village shop in Mayo with a dark drapery counter on one side of it and a bright butcher's counter on the other, and the one girl attending to both: not only does she buy the beasts "on the hoof"—she also kills them herself. "But don't tell anyone that", says she, "or I mightn't get a man." Or it may be just the colour and texture of bread. I have never eaten so many contrasting kinds of home-baked bread since I was a boy in County Down—white "soda" bread, brown wheaten bread, yellow-meal bread, rich dark treacle-bread, rough oatcake, slim fawn potato-farls. If ever the Creator put all his eggs into one basket it was in Down, where the landscape is one of little green elongated hills or "drumlins" whose ups and downs hold continual surprise. But because of their lovely oatmeal texture, their bold contours and colours of gorse, granite, rock and stream, it is the Mourne Mountains, in South Down, that stay most vividly in my memory.

However bright the individual colours in Ireland, however bold the contrast, the grey changing skies and soft muted distance will always discipline them to a reasonable beauty.

"If God had been any good," declared a disgruntled Dubliner on a wet day, "He'd have put a little nip of whisky in the air." Maybe it was as well He didn't. Otherwise what leaning towers, what top-tippling steeples, what rainbow ribbons of talk, what explosive and opposed colours might have flaunted and daunted the air. As it is, there could be no more moderate wish for any man than the old one of "Long life—and death in Ireland!" "The sun", said Turner, "never sets so beautifully as in Ireland." Which doubtless is why so many Irishmen, being dead set against any kind of end, continue to live abroad.

Autumn Scene, on the Dublin-Wicklow
Border

——or anywhere in Ireland, for that matter. The oldest
marks of community in a countryside are its roads, and
the oldest keepers of roads in a country are its "travelling
men" of whom the tinker with his flat cart and barrel-
headed horse-caravan, is the most persistent Irish
representative. The nineteenth century, A.D., brought
compulsory education, in the form of the printed book,
to Ireland and to Europe as a whole; but, for two thousand
years before that, and more, it was the passing traveller
who carried on his tongue's tip the unwritten libraries of
gossip, song, saga, legend, and civilising experience. To
have the story "straight from the horse's mouth" is not
just a racy figure of speech. The oldest peasant story told
orally in the west of Ireland today is one that was told
in Egypt in the nineteenth century B.C. But the tinker is
not to be confused with the gypsy or "Egyptian", though
his origins are prehistoric and mysterious. He is Irish
of the Irish, and always he has exercised a trade, usually
that of smith. "Until recently", says Dr. Evans, "illicit
stills were made and kept in repair by travelling tinkers,
in whom it is perhaps not extravagant to see shades of
the skilled craftsmen of the later Bronze Age who made
cauldrons out of bronze." Tinkers have their own clans,
their own lingo, and they follow their own immemorial
grass roads throughout Ireland.

Photo: Bord Fáilte Éireann

32

Near Costelloe, Connemara

Costelloe is twenty-four miles from Galway City, and nearer still, by fishing-boat, to the Aran Islands. The blue blast from the Atlantic sweeps across the flat expanse of Connemara bog, ruffling the silver mirrors, for, with its many placid loughs, pools, and inlets, this country is essentially a place for reflection. Every cloud, clod, and cow, is doubled. The air is unbelievably clear and clean-washed, and the lovely dilation of distance brings closer the blue mountain masses in the north-west. The high fleecy sky, the black turf-stacks lining the road, the bright outcrops of limestone breaking the skin of grass, the haphazard boulders, the towering quartzite cones of the Twelve Bens (*Beanna Beola*) in the background, make this a memorable and enlarging prospect. Here at last, one feels, there is elbow room and footlooseness.

> *Among these turf-stacks graze no iron horses*
> *Such as stalk such as champ in towns and the soul*
> *of crowds*
> *Here is no mass-production of neat thoughts. . . .*

Because of the constant drift of cloud from the Atlantic the patterns of light are always changing on the land. Colours, too, change. Sometimes the far-off hills look green, sometimes blue or violet or orange-brown, and the gay expansive bog can suddenly contract to a brown study or withdraw into the greyest and most melancholy of moods.

Photo: Bord Fáilte Éireann

Harvesting, near Killarney

The scene might be anywhere in Ireland, from Kerry in the South to Down in the North. A sultry July day of blue sky and high cloud, the green hills beyond, the panting collie dog stretched in the field, the men monotonously shaking out the wind-rows of hay, the salt sweat smarting their eyes and a smoke of flies surrounding them like a halo—how well one knows it all. In Ireland, with its damp climate and rapidly changing weather, it is doubly important to make hay while the sun shines. All hands must help then, even the woman's. And mostly it is handwork, for farms and fields are, by English standards, tiny, so the voice of the combine or the mechanical dryer is seldom heard in the land. The Irish farmer is still very much aware that to manure (*manus*, the hand) a field means in fact, as well as in etymology, to employ the hands. "Are you sure", said a catechising bishop to a West of Ireland peasant, "that there aren't *two* Gods?" "If there is", was the answer, "the second one's name is Manure."

When the hay is "saved" it is put up in cocks or "ricks" which may remain in the field all summer, not from carelessness but because of the variable climate. The little cart (like a slipe on wheels), the dusty grey road, the wild exuberant hedges, all belong to an older world with more leisurely ways and timeless habits.

Photo: Bord Fáilte Éireann

Dunluce Castle

Dunluce (*Dun lios*, the Fort of Enclosures) an Anglo-Norman castle built by Richard de Burgh, Earl of Ulster, about 1300, was taken by the chief of the MacDonnell clan *Somhairle Buidhe* (Yellow Charles) in 1560, who reconstructed it. In the wars with Tudor England, Sorley Boy (as the English colloquially called him) was to prove himself a deep thorn in the flesh of Elizabeth, who alternately wooed and warred with him. Forbidding as his castle, he resisted all political advances. On one occasion Elizabeth sent him documents confirming him in his estates and title as Lord of the Pale. He received the parchment scroll at Dunluce and at once cut it to pieces. "With the sword I won it", he said; "I will never keep it with the sheepskin." But age must give place to progress, and, in his old age, Sorley Boy at Dunluce was sorely reduced by, and submitted carefully to, the English cannon, knowing—as the Irish proverb puts it—that "a chip of the oak splits itself."

Awkward, sinister, and silhouetted against the skyline, Dunluce appears to be part of the high sea rock from which it rises. A giddy footway crosses the ditch (twenty feet broad and a hundred deep) which separates it from the mainland, and under the castle rock runs a cave. In 1639 the kitchen and cooks were suddenly precipitated into the depths, since when the castle has been deserted. Beyond the castle may be seen the White Rocks, part of the limestone formation of County Antrim, in which there are no fewer than twenty-seven caves, some of them extending two miles under the cliff. A blue flower, *Geranium pratense*, which grows abundantly in the neighbourhood, is known as the Flower of Dunluce.

Photo: J. Allan Cash

Cushendun

The quiet coastal road which climbs up from the bay and village of Cushendun has its little hair-raising hills and hairpin drops leading to the most surprising landscape in Antrim, or, indeed, in Ireland. To come unexpectedly upon lovely Murlough Bay with its high green downlands bouncing and bounding steeply to the sea is to be momentarily at a loss for words. To look up at the great basalt pillars of Fairhead (636 feet) is at once to hand over the work of description to a properly equipped nineteenth-century traveller: "The precipice, towering majestic over an awful waste of broken columns, presents to the spectator the most stupendous colonnade ever erected by nature, and in comparison with which the proudest monuments of human architecture are but the efforts of pigmy imbecility to the omnipotence of God."

Cushendun (*Cois-abhann-Duine*, the mouth of the brown river) is, like its handwoven tweeds, an altogether warmer and more human proposition. The village lies at the entrance to Glendun, one of the famed Nine Glens of Antrim. Here, Shane O'Neill, of whom Lord Deputy Sidney complained to Elizabeth that "this man could burn if he liked, up to the gates of Dublin and go away unfought", was murdered in 1567 by the MacDonnells with whom he had sought refuge after defeat. And here Moira O'Neill, the poetess of the Glens, was born. The Glendun River, given a plentiful supply of water, has a good run of sea-trout and salmon in August, and is easily fished: proved sea-trout flies are Blue and Silver, Professor, Peter Ross, and Greenwell. The best of the brown trout fishing is to be found in the upper reaches of the river.

Photo: A. & C. Photography

Glendalough

Glendalough ("glen of the two lakes"), an early monastic settlement in a cup of the Wicklow mountains is impressively lonely and lovely in its setting. The ring of hills, once well-wooded, the bare cone of Camaderry to the right, with its rust-red bracken and scatter of conifers, are unforgettable. "I do not know", said Thackeray, "if there is any tune about Glendalough but, if there be, it must be the most delicate, fantastic, fairy melody that ever was played." But to St. Kevin who founded it in the sixth century, and to his following of anchorites, the tune was a harsh and bitter one. A Leinsterman of noble birth, he chose this place because of its bleak black remoteness. The Irish hermits were as noted for their austerities as for their learning. "My brother," wrote Columcille dryly to Mochua whose only companions, a cock, a mouse, and a fly, had died, "marvel not that thy flock should have died, for misfortune ever waits upon wealth." Here at Glendalough is no rich monastic establishment but the ruins of eight or nine tiny toylike churches, and a round tower once used as a belfry and as a refuge from the Vikings who ravaged the place in the eleventh century. The churches are scattered across the valley for a distance of two miles. Kevin's Bed, a cave above the Upper Lake, is said to have housed the saint for a time, and the little stone hut, known as St. Kevin's cell, may well have been built by him. St. Kevin's Kitchen (*circa* ninth century) is remarkable for its stone roof, most Irish churches of the time being roofed with thatch.

Photo: Bord Fáilte Éireann

O'Connell Bridge, Dublin

O'Connell Bridge, named after the founder of Irish
nationalism, Dan O'Connell, the Liberator (whose statue,
by Foley, appears on the extreme right), is the principal
bridge across the Liffey. Once known as Carlisle Bridge
it was rebuilt in 1794 and again in 1880. Stand long
enough upon it and you will be bound to meet most
Dubliners of your acquaintance, alive or dead, on their
way to the Gaiety theatre or Glasnevin cemetery, for this
bridge is the main life-line between North and South
Dublin. A sea-gull's sweep above it will take in the hub
and hubbub of the city, for here are the principal banks,
the offices of Government, the brewery, the Universities,
the Cathedrals, the excellent restaurants, the theatres,
the fine radio-centre, and the internal terminus for everything. Time and space are joined in one flesh round the
ever-and-nevering nerve of the Liffey, and the feeling of
piety and porter is never far from it. Down river, one
looks towards the North Wall, the departure point for
England and for agonising reappraisal. Up river are the
far reaches of tall painted houses lining the Liffey quays,
steadfastly old and reassuring.

Photo: J. Allan Cash

Meath Hunt (Cubbing Meet)

Sing the peasantry and then
Hard-riding country gentlemen.

County Meath—known as "royal Meath" from its ancient connection with the kings of Tara—is a country of democratically level pastures, royally rich grasslands, slow rivers and humid airs. Its wide fields are necessarily intersected by deep broad ditches for drainage, and these, in all their awkward variety, furnish a God's plenty of exacting jumps for the most cool-headed rider and sure-footed horse. High, overgrown banks of earth contribute to the sporting character of the country. Meath is lacking in the stone walls which are such a feature of the hill country of Ireland, and which represent not so much an enclosure of land as a clearance of rock. Being mostly dry walls, with knock-overable boulders, they make excellent hazards. For centuries the hunt has lent edge and urgency to the quiet fields of Ireland, and horse and rider, and hound, are noted for their endurance. "There was the Scarteen pack of a hundred years ago which hunted as well by night as it did by day and which so little needed guidance of a huntsman that once, says the local legend, the cottagers of the Galtee mountains were startled from their sleep at midnight by the baying of hounds as the Black and Tans swept past on an epic run which carried them thirty miles from the point in Limerick where their huntsman had lost them, and brought them all the way over the Galtees into Tipperary."

Photo: Bord Fáilte Éireann

Ardmore Round Tower, Co. Waterford

Ardmore, with its smooth beach, its colour-washed cottages and green fields is the pleasantest of places. It was once an Episcopal see which for centuries ranked high among the high places of Ireland. For it is said to have been founded by St. Declan who travelled to Rome and returned to Ireland, landing at Ardmore in the year 402, to teach his countrymen the true faith, prior even to the coming of St. Patrick. In one night Declan is supposed to have built the famous Round Tower—the most perfect of its kind in Ireland—and the nearby church, of which the ruins remain. Declan's patron-day, the 24th of July, was for a long time the occasion of a considerable pilgrimage to Ardmore, and his Oratory, a rude hut, is still standing. The Round Tower, originally used as a belfry and refuge, differs from other Irish towers in that it is divided by four beltings, or string courses, into as many stories, with a window-opening to each. It is built of cut stone, is ninety-seven feet high, with a diameter at the base of fifteen feet; the round-headed entrance door is thirteen feet from the ground. The conical cap still stands, but the crutch-like cross which once surmounted it was long ago destroyed by soldiers who used it as a mark for musket-shots.

In 1841, excavations in the base of the Tower revealed the remains of two skeletons, laid in a bed of sifted earth. Above this was a floor of concrete, over which were four successive layers of large stones, closely fitted, and overlaid in turn by a floor of smoothed concrete.

Photo: Bord Fáilte Éireann

Lower Lake, Killarney

To see the landscape of Tuscany for the first time is like looking at the Old Masters; only, they have been cleaned and are life-size. To see the lakes of Killarney for the first time is to realise that this haunting luxuriance of mountain, waterfall, castle, lough, and island has always been part of one's interior landscape, imprinted by nineteenth-century song and canvas; but here it is, now, large and bright as life, strangely familiar.

> *Sweet Inisfallen, long shall dwell*
> *In memory's dream that sunny smile*
> *Which o'er thee on that evening fell,*
> *When first I saw thy fairy isle.*

The view is that of the Lower Lake (Lough Leane) looking towards Tomies Mountain (Mountain of the tumuli or burial cairns). There are some thirty-five islands in this lake, the most notable being Ross and Inisfallen: all are well-wooded. "The arbutus", said Macaulay, "thrives better than even on the sunny shores of Calabria; the turf is of livelier hue than elsewhere; the hills glow with a richer purple, the varnish of the holly and ivy is more glossy, the berries of a brighter red peep through foliage of a brighter green. I never in my life saw anything more beautiful." The Flesk River, a good fishing river, flows into the Lower Lough which is heavily stocked with trout and salmon, the best salmon lures being "Phantom", "Spoon" and "Devon Minnow", with the fly for casting.

Photo: Bord Fáilte Éireann

Carrickfergus Castle

The traditional prophecy, attributed to St. Columba, that "a stranger mounted on a white horse and bearing a shield of painted birds shall conquer Ulster" appeared to be fulfilled when John de Courcy headed the Norman invasion of Ulster in 1177. Gradually the Anglo-Norman overlords established their strongholds along the coastal strip of Ulster, preferring to have outlet to the sea, in case of siege. Their hub of power, Carrickfergus Castle, built between 1180 and 1205, dominated Belfast Lough, the natural point of entry to Ulster. The castle continued for centuries to be the military focus of the North, and wave after wave of native resistance broke against its walls. When in 1210 King John paid a punitive visit to his unruly Anglo-Irish lords in Ulster, it was here he came; the room in which he stayed may still be visited. When Edward Bruce assisted by his brother, King Robert of Scotland, invaded Ireland in 1315, Carrickfergus Castle fell to him after strong resistance, but it reverted to the English after his defeat and death in 1317. In 1688 it was held for James II by Lord Iveagh but was captured the following year by Schomberg. A tablet on the pier below the castle marks the spot where William of Orange first set foot in Ireland in 1690. It is only a few years ago that the castle, for the first time in its history, ceased to house a military garrison. Its most notable feature is the massive square keep, five stories high and with a wall nine feet thick.

Photo: A. & C. Photography

The Clock-gate Tower, Youghal

The Clock Gate, built in 1771, straddles the main street of the pleasant seaport of Youghal in County Cork. Youghal (*Eochaill*, the yew-wood) with its narrow lanes going up and down on either side of the main street, its old grey quays and warehouses, its blue waters and long strand, was a favourite seaside resort for Cork people in Victorian days and is still a popular summer resort. The town is widely known for its association with Sir Walter Raleigh who was sent to Ireland in 1579 to assist in the subjugation of the rebellious Earl of Desmond. Rewarded with 42,000 acres of confiscated land he settled, for some years, at Youghal, and his Elizabethan gabled house, known as Myrtle Grove, may still be seen to the north of the Clock Gate. In the arbour of its garden is the yew-tree under which, it is said, Raleigh smoked the first tobacco brought to Ireland, and read over the manuscript of the *Faerie Queene* at the request of his friend, the poet Spenser, who visited him there. It was to Youghal that "the Shepherd of the seas", as Spenser called him, gratefully diverted on his last "perish or prosper" voyage to South America in 1617. In 1618 Youghal was given an exclusive right to carry on an Irish export trade in woollens. The town was used by John Huston as background for his film-version of *Moby Dick*.

Photo: Bord Fáilte Éireann

Knocknarea, Co. Sligo

West of Sligo town—which, except on the seaward side, is surrounded by mountains—the most striking feature of the landscape is the hill of Knocknarea (1,078 feet). On the south-west of the hill is the Glen of Knocknarea, a deep cleft nearly a mile long and only thirty feet broad, bounded on each side by steep cliffs, and overgrown with trees and shrubs, ferns and ivy, which spring from the crevices in the rock; a botanist's paradise. Topping the wide and windy hill is a great cairn known as *Miscaun Meadhbh*, reputedly a monument to Queen Maeve of Connaught who flourished in the first century of the Christian era: it was this Maeve who, to capture the Brown Bull of Cooley, incited the rest of Ireland to attack Ulster. The cairn has a circumference of 630 feet at the base, the slope to the crown being 80 feet and the diameter on the top 100 feet; and the weight of stones used has been estimated at 40,000 tons. These mysterious monuments of prehistoric builders, the megalithic grave, dolmen, cairn, sprinkle the high places of County Sligo. All this countryside is neck-deep in the remains of unrecorded history. It moved the imagination of Yeats in his poem about resurgent Ireland:

The wind has bundled up the clouds high over Knocknarea,
And thrown the thunder on the stones for all that Maeve
  can say,
Angers that are like noisy clouds have set our hearts abeat;
But we have all bent low and low and kissed the quiet feet
Of Cathleen, the daughter of Houlihan.

Photo: Bord Fáilte Éireann

Enniskillen

Enniskillen (*Inis Ceitleann*, Ceithle's Island) the capital of County Fermanagh illustrates very well the long, neat, narrow street of the Northern Irish agricultural town. It stands on the winding River Erne between Upper and Lower Lough Erne. At this strategic bridgehead the Maguires, turbulent lords of Fermanagh, built their castle, and the remains of the fifteenth-century keep may still be seen. In the sixteenth century, when the lord-deputy of Ireland sent word that he was about to send a sheriff into the district, the Maguire replied that "her majesty's officer would be received; but at the same time he desired to know his *eric*—the fine to be imposed on his murderer." The Maguire stronghold was confiscated by the Crown in the following century and awarded to Sir William Cole who settled it with twenty English families and defended it in the war of 1641. The town continued to be stubbornly disputed, and in 1689 the Garrison decisively defeated an attacking Jacobite force of twice its number. Song and story have ever since celebrated two of the oldest and most famous of British regiments, the Inniskilling Fusiliers and the Inniskilling Dragoons— *The Skins*—whose home-link is with Enniskillen. At the Battle of the Boyne (1690) William of Orange led *the ould Skins* in person. "Gentlemen," he said, at the height of the battle, "you shall be my guards this day. I have heard much of you." Tradition says that, earlier, the Jacobite troops had almost surprised the sleeping troops of William when suddenly a little bird alighted on the drum of an Inniskilling lad and proceeded to tap out the alarm which saved the day. How neatly tradition telescopes the *Skin* and the drum-skin!

Enniskillen dominates one of the loveliest lakes in Europe on whose shore is the famous Portora Royal School where Oscar Wilde was educated.

Photo: J. Allan Cash

Minaun Cliffs, Achill, Co. Mayo

"On no occasion", wrote a traveller, approaching Achill a century ago, "have we so completely felt our utter inability to render justice to the wonderful works of Nature." Achill, approached today by an iron bridge across the Sound, is the largest island off the Irish coast. Shaped like an inverted L, it is fifteen miles in length, its greatest width being twelve miles. For the most part its wide heathery turf and bare windy mountains are walled with magnificent sea-cliffs and swathed with soft Atlantic rains, so that sometimes one feels that it is hardly worth a day's while to get dry here. But on a golden rain-washed morning of blue sky, purple shadows and lazy sea it becomes a land of great distances and incisive beauty, and its many warm scattered villages hum with summer visitors. Ireland has much fine cliff-scenery—Fair Head in Antrim, Slieve League in Donegal, the Cliffs of Moher in Clare—but none finer than the cliffs of Minaun (*Cnoc Mo-Fionnain*, the Mountain of St. Finnan) on Achill. These may best be seen, and approached by foot, from the village of Keel which lies at the western end of Tramore Strand, a curve of firm sand that runs for two miles towards them. The Minaun Cliffs, which fall 800 feet to the sea, have been weathered into queer quartzite shapes, the most fantastic of which are the "Cathedral Rocks" at the northern extremity. The cliffs of Achill were the last haunts of the golden eagle in these parts.

Photo: Bord Fáilte Éireann

Near Buncrana, Donegal

Gay sunlights o'er the hillocks creep
And join for golden weather,—
A scythe-sweep, and a scythe-sweep,
We mow the dale together.

In mountainy parts of Donegal where small pockets of corn ripen among stone and heather one may see even the sickle at work, for Donegal is a county of great littlenesses of field and fold, and immense patchwork variety. Our picture, taken near Buncrana in the barony of Inishowen, shows a shapely hill or "drumlin" in the middle distance. Ulster has a greater swarm of these drumlins—streamlined deposits of boulder clay carried there by glaciers in the Ice Age—than any other country, and they form most valuable farming land. Of all the Irish counties Donegal is, to my mind, the loveliest, and the mountainous peninsula of Inishowen, dominated by Slieve Snacht, one of its loveliest parts. This territory was once owned by the O'Dohertys, and even today, as the saying goes— "you can't beat a bush in Inishowen without 'rising' an O'Doherty." The family seat of Sir Cahir O'Doherty, the last proud lord of the clan may still be seen at Buncrana. It was he who, with Spanish hat and high heron feather, sacked and burned Derry whose governor had insulted him; his fatal action led to the Plantation of Ulster by the English and Scotch settlers of James I.

To the left may be seen Lough Swilly from which, in 1607, the last of the Irish Earls set sail for the Continent. Here too, in 1798, the English fleet brought the captured French battleship *Hoche*, with Wolfe Tone, the ill-fated Irish patriot, on board.

Photo: Bord Fáilte Éireann

Errigal and the Dunlewy River

Errigal (2,466 feet) is the tallest peak in the ice-carved Donegal highlands. With its furrowed sides and white screes of broken quartz it is far and away the finest of all conical mountains in Ireland. It is best approached by way of Dunlewy, and one way up is as good as another. There are, in fact, two tops to Errigal, a quarter of a mile apart. Between them runs the narrow, giddy One Man's Path. On a clear day the view from the highest point—no bigger than a little table—is gloriously wild. Immediately below are the immense tracts of rolling moorland, the corrie called The Poisoned Glen (because of the spurge which supposedly poisons its waters) and the Slieve Snacht range. Beyond are the many lakes and hills of Donegal, and all the lovely indented coastline. Knocklayd in Antrim, and Benbulben in Sligo, are hints on the horizon.

But it is the view of Errigal itself, in its blaze of white and blue, that draws the visitor and the artist. "He's pulling Errigal", explained one Donegal child to another, watching an artist at work sketching the peak. The puzzled artist suddenly remembered that the child was a Gaelic speaker for whom the alien words "drawing" and "pulling" were synonymous.

The hard quartzite rock, in contradistinction to the softer granites and shales, has given bold and lasting outline to peaks like Errigal, Muckish, or the Great Sugarloaf of the Wicklow Mountains.

Photo: A. & C. Photography

Greystones, Co. Wicklow

County Wicklow, with its moorland wastes and bare granite hills has a wealth of lovely valley, wooded glen, and smoking waterfall. Dean Swift likened it to "a frieze mantle fringed with gold lace". Much of the coastland is low, being a drift-covered plain, fringed from Wicklow to near Greystones by a shingle bank known as "The Murrough", but the ancient quartzites rise westwards to form the fine conical hills of the Great Sugarloaf (1,659 feet) and the Little Sugarloaf. Greystones, a quiet holiday resort and residential district, lies in a pleasantly wooded part of the Wicklow coast, a few miles south of Bray Head, and eighteen miles from Dublin. It retains in part the atmosphere of the former fishing village, and at the same time its wide tree-fringed roads, well-trimmed hedges and modern residences are an example of town-planning at its best. Holiday-makers in Ireland may safely be divided into those who like the respectable urban amenities of an East coast town with sandy beach, cinema, badminton, excellent eighteen-hole golf course, and those who prefer the exuberant rough-and-tumble of the stony coastal parts of the West. There could, I think, be no greater contrast than that between Greystones, in County Wicklow, and Roundstone, in County Galway. But Greystones has unquestionably this advantage—it lies within the dry coastal strip of the East where the annual rainfall is a mere thirty to forty inches and the average summer temperature is just under sixty degrees, and the town has easy access to Wicklow's finest scenery.

Photo: Bord Fáilte Éireann

Narrow Water Castle

Narrow Water Castle at the bottle-neck of the Newry Water which runs into Carlingford Lough was built after the restoration of Charles II, to protect the commercial town of Newry and its strategic hinterland of Down, Armagh, and Louth. It stands on the site of a thirteenth-century stronghold which, like Newry, was destroyed in the Great War of 1641. The lovely shores of Carlingford Lough (*Carline-fiord*) are dotted with the names and claims of successive invaders. Megalithic man, Dane, Norman and Saxon, all entered Ulster by way of this narrow inlet, and the distinctive Horned Cairns of Ulster, raised two thousand years ago and more, are part of what is known to archaeologists as the Carlingford Culture. From the fine wooded slopes behind the Castle one looks south across the narrow water to the purple mountains of Louth and the rocky headland of Cooley, which, though not a part of Ulster, was once the fiefdom of her greatest hero, Cuchulain, when Ulster was ruled by the Red Branch Circle of pagan warriors. The oldest and best of all Celtic sagas, *Tain-Bo-Cuailgne*, tells of the great raid made upon Ulster by the rest of Ireland in order to capture the Brown Bull of Cooley, and of how Cuchulain defeated the invaders. Today the narrow water, 300 yards wide, separates political Ulster from the Republic of Ireland, but not a few Irish bulls have managed to make their way north by night across this narrow water of the Border, to reinstate the customary Ireland against the Ireland of Customs and Excise.

Photo: A. & C. Photography

Clogherhead, Co. Louth

Louth, the smallest of the Irish counties, lying between the Boyne Estuary and Carlingford Lough, bulks largely in Irish history, for it was always a border country and debatable land. It guarded the Gap of the North, the pass that runs from the plains of Leinster into the hills of Ulster. Here Cuchulain, the champion of Ulster when Ulster had a pagan chivalry, had his first-century stronghold. At the Boyne River, the decisive battle between James II and William III took place in 1690. Brigid, "mother of all the saints of Ireland"—"Mary of the Gael"—was born in County Louth in the fifth century. It is a highly-cultivated, fertile county of undulating pastures but it has also its long sandy beaches and quiet fishing villages like Clogher. Clogher—with Clogher Head (183 feet) behind it—is a pleasant straggle of white-washed cottages going down to the sea. On the north side, about a mile away over the hill, is the harbour; and the dune-backed strand stretches for a mile and a half. Visitors from Drogheda, nine miles distant, come here for fishing and bathing in the summer months. In winter this Irish Sea can be remarkably rough and unaccommodating, reminding one of Oliver Cromwell whose indiscriminate massacre of the population of Drogheda has made his memory a by-word in Ireland. Tradition ascribes the roughness of the Irish Sea to Cromwell's coffin, doomed to toss restlessly to and fro between England and Ireland, eschewed by both countries.

Photo: Bord Fáilte Éireann

Mourne Mountains

It was in the Mournes I learned that there is no better way of getting to know the nerve of a mountain than by walking up a stream to its source. And by that I mean walking *in* the stream. Every step is a watery one, and every stone is a friend, and the goose-flesh of Mourne granite is a friend indeed to the slippery bare foot. Shallow rapids, ferny clefts, deep dark peat-brown pools, flashing tails of spray—all take on a new inward look.

There was Bloody River
Where the granite pickles bristled and blazed, and
Ebullient water bellied over
Boulders with the sweep of a bell's shoulders.

The nice thing about stream-climbing is that it can be done pleasurably on a rainy day, for there is a point at which wetness ceases to matter and becomes exhilarating. But a blazing day is perfect for the job, and if you carry a geological ordnance survey map there is the added pleasure of maybe finding a vein of greenstone or a band of diorite that has not been marked on the map.

Our picture is of the Central Mournes seen from above Hilltown where the infant River Bann begins to put on weight. Above Hilltown it is of no great account so far as angling is concerned, though it furnishes ideal spawning beds. But below Hilltown there are many fine—and free —reaches where brown trout may be taken. Indeed the Upper Bann is one of the best trout streams in Northern Ireland.

Photo: J. Allan Cash

Cottage in County Clare

The cottage, thatched and white-washed, fits the Irish landscape perfectly. It is as much part and parcel of it as the limestone walls that enclose the fields. Simple in design it is the product of a highly intricate peasant mind with long and cultivated traditions. It is "unlucky" to widen a house, therefore the cottage is enlarged by lengthwise additions which somewhat obscure its original feature, that of the one-roomed cabin with either a central or an end hearth. No Irish cottage would be complete without

> . . . . *the peeping of things*
> *Across the half-door*

which lends light and airiness to the work of the household. Always, too, there is a back door for use when the wind is on the front of the house, and for access to cattle and poultry. Old beliefs and taboos have attached themselves to the proper use of these doors. I know no cosier sight than the neat kitchen of a Clare cottage, with its open hearth and turf fire, its dresser hung with flowered jugs and brown-and-blue striped mugs, its Brigid's Cross on the raftered ceiling, and its always-burning candle. On a winter's night, when neighbours gather in to gossip, there is song and dance to a tin whistle and fascinating stories of old times and people, and of the dangers of lonely places. "It has to do with the host", explained a Clareman to me, meaning the faery host. "We are surrounded by listening people."

Photo: J. Allan Cash

Brandon Peak

Mount Brandon (3,127 feet), in the Dingle peninsula, the second highest peak in Ireland, has long been associated with Brendan ("the Navigator") the sixth-century Irish saint whose first foundation it was. On his feast day, the 16th of May, pilgrims climb the Saint's Road to the summit where the ruins of Brendan's Oratory may be seen. "When he was here with us in Kerry", a country-woman explained to me, "he used to say a special Mass every Sunday and holy day on top of the mountain. He would give a big long sermon and instruction to the people who followed him about. One day he forgot the Mass-book. He looked over his shoulder at the clerk who was standing beside him and spoke to him in a low voice. He told him he had left the book behind him at Kilmalkedar Chapel. The clerk spoke to the man nearest to him, and if he did, no one stirred. Of the big crowd that was following St. Brendan that Easter Sunday not one of them turned about or moved a foot. But from mouth to mouth the word went till it reached the bottom of the hill. A messenger went to Kil Chapel where St. Brendan had his old church, and got the book. And, when he came to where the end of the procession of people was, he stretched the book from him to one of them, and the book went from hand to hand, with no one leaving his place until the holy saint got the book into his own hand at the altar on top of the hill."

Photo: J. Allan Cash

Brandon Bay, Co. Kerry

Mount Brandon, austere and impressive at all times, cloudy at most times, dominates Brandon Bay across whose waters the light and biddable curraghs—lath-and-canvas canoes—have bounded for a millennium and more. It was from this bay, they say, that St. Brendan and his monks set out on their epic voyage into the Atlantic in the year 551, a journey which formed the basis of the mediaeval legend of the *Navigation of St. Brendan*. Sailing in search of an earthly Paradise he had many unearthly adventures. In the northern seas he came upon a floating mountain— "the colour of silver, harder than marble, of substance of the clearest crystal"; an iceberg, in fact. There were strange sea-beasts with "cat-like heads, eyes of the colour of a bronze cauldron, fuzzy pelts, boars' tusks and heavy spotted bellies". On Christmas night he met Judas who once a year was allowed to cool himself on a lonely rock in return for a single act of charity done in his lifetime. After forty days Brendan and his companions sailed southwards through a sea which "had thrice fifty islands, and some thrice the size of Eire" to "a land, odorous, flower-smooth, blessed; a land many-melodied, musical, shouting for joy, unmournful", finding there a hermit, the last survivor of a Celtic Christian community which had preceded him by fifty years. Was it the New World he reached? And was that its first recorded touch with Europe? And did he return fondly to the dark bare mountain that dominated Brandon Bay, "but no longer at ease here, in the old dispensation"?

Photo: Bord Fáilte Éireann

Custom House, Dublin

The Custom House, erected between the years 1781 and 1791, at a cost of £546,000, is the finest public building in Dublin; it represents the flowering of Dublin commerce and Irish parliamentary power in the eighteenth century. James Gandon, whose masterpiece it was, and who helped to make Dublin a capital rather than a provincial city, was brought from England by John Beresford the Banker. Here too, enlarging influences were at work, for Gandon, English-born of Huguenot parentage, was the pupil of a Scot who had studied in Rome. Invited by Princess Dashkoff to go to Petrograd he chose to settle in Dublin, and the Custom House is, in the words of an English critic, "as different from London as though it had risen on the banks of the Neva." Built by Irish artificers and decorated by the greatest of Irish sculptors, it has, on the main river front, a fine Doric portico with allegorical figures. Flanking each of the wings is a pavilion with the arms of Ireland above. A superb dome, topped by a statue of Hope resting on her anchor, surmounts the whole.

In the foreground of the picture may be aptly seen the *Lady Grania*, belonging to the fleet of Guinness whose product has brought both fame and revenue to Dublin. A far cry, indeed, from the eighteenth-century "Irish Navy" which, it is estimated, consisted of some four hundred smuggling vessels carrying wines and brandies to the West of Ireland from the Continent and America, and patronised, if not subsidised, by the best Irish families.

Photo: Bord Fáilte Éireann

Rossnowlagh, Co. Donegal

"Praise the beach when you come to it", runs the Gaelic saying, and Rossnowlagh (*the Wood of the Apples*) is entirely praiseworthy. Donegal, with its thousand tongues stuck out at the sea, has more than its fair share of fine bays and creeks and beaches. It is a tantalising county to travel in, for one is always tempted to go to extremes and to neb-ends of peninsulas in the hope of finding yet another lonely tawny strand tucked deeply away under cliffs or dunes. Some of these strands, popular in summer, are so long that the motor cars huddle together in one place for fear of losing themselves.

Rossnowlagh, a seaside resort five miles north of Ballyshannon, has one of the finest strands in Ireland. It fronts a wide reach of level sward hemmed in by gentle hills, and it faces the blue Atlantic where it rolls into the long sweep of Donegal Bay. It was of this coast that William Allingham sang in his famous ballad "Adieu to Ballyshannon".

> *Farewell to you, Kildoney lads, and them that pull an oar,*
> *A lug-sail set, or haul a net, from the Point to*
> *   Mullaghmore,*
> *From Killybegs to bold Slieve-League, that ocean-*
> *   mountain steep,*
> *Six hundred yards in air aloft, six hundred in the deep;*
> *From Dooran to the Fairy Bridge, and round by Tullen*
> *   strand,*
> *Level and long, and white with waves, where gull and*
> *   curlew stand,——*
> *Head out to sea when on your lee the breakers you*
> *   discern——*
> *Adieu to all the billowy coast, and winding banks of Erne!*

Photo: Bord Fáilte Éireann

Golf at Killarney

The Lakes of Killarney have long been praised for their beauty. "As for a man coming from his desk in London or Dublin", said Thackeray, "and seeing 'the whole lakes in a day', he is an ass for his pains. We should look at these wonderful things leisurely and thoughtfully." There can be no more leisurely, thoughtful, or oblique way of enjoying Killarney "in little" than a day spent in golfing there. Killarney Golf Course (eighteen holes S.S.S. 75) is a proper championship course in every respect. In 1949 and 1953 the Irish Open Amateur Championship was held there, and Killarney was also the venue for the 1953 Home Internationals and Walker Cup Trial. It is said to be the only genuine "lake-side" golf course in the world, combining the hazardous virtues of the seaside and the inland. The new Killarney Course, on the northern shores of Lough Leane, was opened in 1939 and is up-to-date in design. Through a system of alternative tees—championship, medal, and forward—it possesses, in effect, three courses in one. But whether the golfer chooses the pushed-back or forward tees, whether he plays "tiger" golf, or plain bread-and-butter golf, he is assured of a landscape setting that is unequalled anywhere. Still, the view must not detract from the game, and a noted English match player once informed me that the thing which most impressed him about his Irish opponents was their will to win and their spirit of attack in all circumstances.

Photo: J. Allan Cash

Inistioge, Co. Kilkenny

Inistioge ("Teoc's or Tighe's Island") is a most pleasant example of the little Irish village with church, cross, spirit-grocery, petrol-pump grouped round a quiet shadowy square. Time stands still, and the children under the lime-trees wait happily for the bus that has forgotten to come. The village lies in the prettiest part of the lovely Nore Valley on the west bank of the Nore, a good trout and salmon river.

The stubborn Newre, whose waters grey
By fair Kilkenny and Ross-ponte board,

as Spenser described it. It is here crossed by an old and elegantly-arched bridge, ornamented on the southern side by Ionic pillars. Two ancient towers, one of them incorporated in the clock-faced parish church, recall the Austin friary that was founded in 1210. A ruined Norman fort overlooks the river, and far to the east is the rounded head of Mount Brandon. Nearby is the once-famous and finely-wooded demesne of Woodstock, formerly the home of the Tighe family. "It is impossible", wrote a nineteenth-century traveller, "to render justice to this fascinating place."

Here in this happy Eden of our earth,
Dwelling with Nature and her holy train,
A mortal woman gave a spirit birth,
And Psyche made immortal once again.

Flaxman's effigy of the poetess, Mrs. Mary Tighe (died 1810), authoress of "Psyche", may be seen in one of the village churches.

Photo: Bord Fáilte Éireann

Derryclare Lough, Connemara

"One of the most wild and beautiful districts that it is ever the fortune of the traveller to examine; and I could not help thinking as we passed through it", said Thackeray, "how much pain and expense honest English cockneys are at to go and look after natural beauties far inferior, in countries which, though more distant, are not a whit more strange than this one." Derryclare Lough is in the heart of the Connemara country, in the part of County Galway which lies between Lough Corrib and the Atlantic. Beyond it rises the finest of all mountain ridges, that of the Twelve Bens with their cone-shaped quartzite peaks, each one distinct and lovely in its own right. A good country for botanists, for the steep slopes are richly coloured with lichens and mosses. Many of the countryfolk are Irish speakers and students of the language come here to learn it. Derryclare Lough forms part of the famous salmon fishery of Ballynahinch. Beside the lough the finest Connemara marble is quarried. Connemara, indeed, has long been known for the quality of its stone. "Precious serpentine", reported a nineteenth-century traveller, "of various shades of green and yellow, often mottled and striped, is intermixed with the white and rose-coloured limestones; and a very beautiful marble is produced, precisely the same in structure and appearance as the *verde antico* of Italy, and undoubtedly the richest and finest ornamental stone yet found in these islands."

Photo: J. Allan Cash

General View of Carlow

The county of Carlow was made shire-ground by King John, under the name of Catherlogh ("the castle by the lake"). The town of Carlow is finely placed in the fertile limestone valley of the deep, slow river Barrow, the "goodlie Barrow", as Spenser called it, which for centuries separated the English Pale from the restless Irish clans. Here, where a tributary, the Burren, joins the Barrow, a four-angled lake is formed, which gave name and strategic importance to the town. Most prominent is the Anglo-Norman castle on the east bank, built, probably, by Hugh de Lacy, Lord Deputy of Ireland, in 1180. It dominated the approach to the Pale. Norman, Saxon, and Gael fought bloodily for it, throughout the centuries, without substantial damage to its structure. But in 1814 it came into the hands of a local doctor who, to make the walls more thin-skinned for his insane patients, set explosives in the foundations: he succeeded in blowing most of the castle to pieces. Only the west wall and flanking tower remain.

"Low steeple, arrogant people", runs the old Carlow jest, for the district was once "studded with the seats of resident gentry." The Parish church has, in fact, a graceful spire, and the Catholic cathedral has three fine stained-glass windows by Harry Clarke. The Old Assembly Rooms were presented to the town by Bernard Shaw who had family connections with Carlow.

Photo: Bord Fáilte Éireann

Carnlough, from the South

Groined by deep glens and walled along the west
by the bare hilltops and the tufted moors,
this rim of arable that ends in foam. . . .

The lovely Nine Glens bite deeply into the basalts of the Antrim plateau and into the hard overlays of modern history. Cut off, until a century ago, by land barriers, these green pockets of Gaelic life have kept their own distinct tradition and character. Their outlook was always towards Scotland, whose white-washed houses may be seen on clear days across the Stream of the Moyle; and their turbulent lords, the MacDonnells, were also Lords of the Isles. Since the opening of the fine coast road, designed by Lanyon in 1834, the little harbours at the mouths of the glens have grown to seaside resorts, and Carnlough, at the foot of Glencloy, has its ribbon-development and its straggle of caravans today. George Shiels, the Ulster playwright, lived here, and Sir Winston Churchill owned house property which, between the wars, he gave to the occupiers. To the north of the bay is Garron Point, near to which is the rock of Dunmaul, anciently fortified. Tradition says that in olden times all the rents of Ireland were paid at this place, and from it the last Danish invaders embarked. A number of small mountain lakes behind Carnlough offer good trout fishing.

Photo: A. & C. Photography

Ballynahinch River

In a superb setting of mountains—the Twelve Bens of Connemara—lies Ballynahinch Lake which forms part of the famous Ballynahinch fishery. A fine salmon-river empties the lake into a creek of Bertraghboy Bay. The main road from Recess to Clifden runs alongside, under the shadow of Ben Lettery. The west of Ireland is not the driest of places; but it is an ill wind that blows nobody good and proper, and the angler here can be thankful for a ready downpour. These western rivers rise rapidly after heavy rain, and a dry season is the death of them. Nothing is more enlivening than the sight of a salmon-river at the tail-end of a flood with the glint of fish in it. Ballynahinch Lake, though mainly noted for the excellence of its sea-trout, is well stocked with grilse in the summer months. On its southern shore is Ballynahinch Castle, now an hotel, which for long was the home of the Martin family which settled in Galway in the thirteenth century. Its most notable member was Richard Martin, friend of George IV. Known to his tenants as "The King of Connemara" and to the world at large as "Humanity Dick" (he was a founder of the Royal Society for the Prevention of Cruelty to Animals) he ruled feudally a vast estate of 197,000 acres. Maria Edgeworth visited this elegant house, and Thackeray too came as a guest here, went on a fishing expedition, ate fine salmon trout, and saw "a real wild eagle".

Photo: J. Allan Cash

94

Ardglass

Ardglass (*Ard glas*, the green height), a fishing town in County Down, lies opposite to the Isle of Man, and is one of the nearest points to any English seaport. It early became an English settlement therefore, and stayed so at a time when English influence had otherwise ebbed from Ulster. In mediaeval days it was the principal trading port of Down, doing business with England and the Continent. Like many other merchant towns of the period it was protected by "castles"—five in all—which were, in fact, half fortress and half warehouse. We are told that they formed part of a long range of "booths" for the sale of merchandise, open towards the land for the purpose of trade, and having loopholes towards the sea with a view to defence. Of these, a few remain, in various stages of decay, adaptation, or preservation. Shane's Castle, which overlooks the bay, is thought to have been built by a trading company in the reign of Henry IV. Jordan's Castle, in the middle of the town, was built in the fifteenth century and is the best preserved. It takes its name from Simon Jordan, a sixteenth-century merchant who held it for three years against Hugh O'Neill, Earl of Tyrone.

Today, Ardglass is a pleasant fishing port used by herring-boats of many nationalities. Everyone born in rural Ulster knows the sound of the fish-pedlar's cart and the cry of "Fresh herrin', the day! Fresh herrin'! Ardglass herrin'!"

Photo: A. & C. Photography

Desmond Castle, Adare

On the road from Limerick to Killarney is Adare (*Ath Dara*, the ford of the oaks) on the river Maigue. In its well-wooded setting, with mediaeval church ruins and neat thatched cottages, it is a surprisingly lovely village. Once an O'Donovan stronghold, it was taken by the Anglo-Normans in the reign of Henry II. In 1227 the O'Donovan castle passed into the hands of the Fitzgeralds, earls of Kildare, who rebuilt and strengthened it in the following century. Burned by Turlogh O'Brien in the fifteenth century it was again restored, but in 1534 it fell forfeit to the Crown because of Fitzgerald support for the pretender, Perkin Warbeck. The Earl of Desmond, kinsman to the Fitzgerald, leased the castle and estates from the Crown, but the Desmonds were, in turn, crushed and their lands confiscated in Elizabethan times. All this territory is studded with the impressive remains, monastic and castellated, of the Desmond family, of whom Macaulay wrote that "they were the greatest and proudest subjects that any Sovereign of Europe ever had." Gerald, the sixteenth Earl of Desmond, figures largely in the Elizabethan wars as *ingens rebellibus exemplar*. He possessed, says a chronicler, "whole countries, together with the county Palatine of Kerry, and had, of his own name and race, at least 500 gentlemen at his command, all of whom, and his own life also, he lost within the space of three years. His vast estate was a strong inducement to the chief governors of Ireland to make or proclaim him a rebel." The fortunes of Spenser, Raleigh, Boyle, and a host of English adventurers, were founded on Desmond's ruin.

St. Finbarr's Cathedral and River Lee, Cork City

Cork, the chief city of Munster, is said to have been founded in the sixth or seventh century by a Connaught-man, St. Finbarr, who established a monastic settlement containing no fewer than 700 priests, monks and students, on the south side of the River Lee. Dane and Anglo-Norman in turn ravaged the place and established trading centres there. In the seventeenth century, tradesmen from half the ports in Europe came to Cork for salt fish, salt butter and salt meat. St. Finbarr's Cathedral, the most notable building in Cork, is comparatively modern. The original church, on whose site it stands, was destroyed in the Williamite siege of 1690; only a cannon-ball remains, hanging in the transept of the present church, as witness. The poet, Edmund Spenser, who was probably married in the old church described

The spreading Lee, that, like an island fayre,
Encloseth Cork with his divided flood.

The Lee—the Luvius of Ptolemy—from its mouth to its source in the lake of Gougane Barra, a distance of fifty-five miles, is one of the most delightful rivers in Ireland, its winding course dotted with the ruins of castle, abbey, and monastery. And Gougane Barra in its amphi-theatre of hills is startlingly beautiful. On a pilgrim island in the lake are the ruined oratory and chapel of Finbarr who lived here previous to his founding the Cathedral in Cork.

Photo: Bord Fáilte Éireann

100

Tyrella

Tyrella is largely a point of view. But a superb view, for, from the long bathing strand, one looks southward across the Bay of Dundrum to where the Mountains of Mourne roll down to the sea in slow, rounded procession. "What the day has in mind the mountain knows about", and the granite domes of the Mournes are good weather gauges; sometimes swathed to the knees in cloud, sometimes green and gay and glittering with wet scree, scar, rusty bracken or purple heather. But, seen from any angle, that clear-cut profile of hills, falling away seawards like a fading drum-roll, is unmistakably Mourne. "Friendly Mourne", it is called, not only because of its gently persuasive contours but because of its people who are as rounded as the hills they live among. For the Mourne man is farmer, fisherman, stone-cutter, and shepherd, all rolled into one, and he has the hard sparkle of his native granite. To lie in the heather on a hot day and to listen to the stony chatter of his chisel, or to watch him, when building a house, climb the hillside behind it and fix his roof-level against that of the sea's horizon, is to know that here is a craftsman who has been soundly shaped by his environment. The "kingdom of Mourne" lies off the main traffic routes and was, for centuries, relatively inaccessible, so it has preserved older ways of life more than most parts of Ulster. And because it has its own hub of history and custom, instead of an urban hubbub, it has a family air and intimacy about it which draw visitors warmly back to it, year after year.

Photo: A. & C. Photography

Harvesting, Co. Sligo

Hay-harvesting is later in Ireland than in England because of the cooler summers and humid climate, and for the same reason the haycock is a notable feature of the Irish fields where it often lingers until the dry autumn months before it is safely housed.

In the background of this harvesting scene is King's Mountain (1,527 feet) forming part of the Benbulben plateau which in turn forms part of the Dartry Mountains

Under bare Ben Bulben's head,
In Drumcliff churchyard, Yeats is laid.

W. B. Yeats, the poet, wandered this Sligo countryside as a youth, and its sights and sounds and names figure famously in his poetry—Lissadell, Drumnahair, Innisfree, Knocknarea, The Rosses. Everywhere, for miles around, the great limestone bulk of the Benbulben plateau faces the traveller inescapably. Its high cheek-bones, its flattened top, its boldly-changing contour, sometimes seen hull-on, sometimes broadside, like a ship riding the green wave of the fields, make it unforgettable. It ends abruptly and dramatically, four miles from the Atlantic.

Benbulben is known among botanists for its rare flora, including *Arenaria ciliata* and *Saxifraga nivalis*. One of the most famous of Irish legends and love-tales which tells of the successful flight and epic pursuit of Diarmuid and Grainne, the eloping lovers, had its resolution on the slopes of this mountain where Diarmuid was killed while taking part in a boar-hunt.

Photo: Bord Fáilte Éireann

Rossbeigh, Co. Kerry

Kerry has a clean beauty of bone about it denied to the other more fleshy counties of Ireland, for although this south-west corner was notably glaciated in the Ice Age it was not overcoated by Drift to the same extent. Clear hard outlines and boldly-drawn distances mark this county, which looks as if it had been designed in one of God's more expansive moods. From the shadow of Curra Hill (*currac cinn adhmuid*) we have a bird's eye view of the vast sweep of Dingle Bay, with the Dingle Mountains beyond. Immediately below us is Rossbeigh Strand, mile upon empty mile of fine bathing beach, backed by sandhills. Here John Synge, the dramatist, watched the horse-racing on the sands and listened to an old man tell tales of Tir-na-nOg, the land of Eternal Youth. "'The Tir-na-nOg itself', he said, 'is below that sea, and a while since there were two men out in a boat in the night-time, and they got stuck outside some way or another. They went to sleep then, and when one of them wakened up he looked down into the sea, and he saw the Tir-na-nOg and people walking about, and side-cars driving in the squares'."

Nearby, where the Behy river enters Dingle Bay, is the village of Glenbeigh, nestling at the foot of Seefin Mountain. Diarmuid, one of the heroes of Irish saga, fished for salmon in this river, on his epic flight with Grania, his lover. It is still a fine—and free—fishing river with sea-trout (after a flood) and grilse.

Photo: Bord Fáilte Éireann

Killarney Races

Lying at the foot of Torc Mountain (on the extreme left), and ringed by hill and lake, Killarney Racecourse has the best scenic setting in these islands. The races, held in July of each year, are noted for large entries and large crowds. Every Irishman has a race in his blood even if he hasn't a horse in his paddock. "If they have three acres," complained a Government Report of last century, "they think they must have a horse", and "Bred in Ireland" has been the hallmark of many a winner at Ascot or Belmont Park. All roads lead to loam, and the limestone pastures of Ireland are second to none—not even to the renowned "Blue Grass" region of Kentucky—in their bone-building properties. A day of blue sky, breezy cloud, fluttering flags, excited people, glossy horses pounding the turf— what could be more convivial? Or what more admirable than the proud horse that is led in by his owner? I have known, indeed, an owner (who had celebrated too previously) to be led in by his horse. But Irish races, after all, are sociable events.

> *It's there you'd see the jockeys and they mounted on*
>   *most stately*
> *The pink and blue, the red and green, the Emblem of*
>   *our nation.*
> *When the bell was rung for starting, all the horses*
>   *seemed impatient,*
> *I thought they never stood on ground, their speed was*
>   *so amazing.*
> *There was half a million people there of all*
>   *denominations,*
> *The Catholic, the Protestant, the Jew and Presbyterian.*
> *There was yet no animosity, no matter what persuasion,*
> *But fáilte and hospitality inducing fresh acquaintance.*

Waggon-families, at Puck Fair

The Irishman has always (like a walking stick) leafy visions of settling down and taking root. But his dearest wish is to be "on the move", or "on the run". Which, no doubt, is why he is mighty tolerant of the travelling people, of the gypsy and the tinker. No fair-day or market-day in Ireland would be complete without the presence of the tinker who represents everything that is free, foot-loose, and elusive within an ordered, settled, and watchful community. The oldest and greatest annual foregathering of tinkers is always at Puck Fair, Killorglin, County Kerry. To know why, would be to know better the course of Irish character and history. But, there it is! "Beyond the Leap, beyond the law". For days their gaily coloured waggons line the approach to this law-abiding but waiting-to-be-titillated town. A kaleidoscope of tousled children, dogs, piebald ponies and foals, fills the road. And (let me say) their caravans are as shining and neat as new pins. Their trades may range from mending tin kettles to buying horses, at which they are traditionally adept. They are curiously gentle, reserved, people, yet—amongst themselves—they are the fiercest fighters, and have the lowest flash point, in Ireland. Wards, Tuohys, Sullivans, Collins, Coffees—all the tinker tribes —have their internecine feuds, and the whiff of a bottle of whisky is enough to waken them. And, since they harm no one but themselves, and are a shockingly good example to everyone, the Law turns a blind and fond eye to their nice idiosyncracies.

Photo: Inge Morath